THE WOMAN'S WAY

✛

TIME®
LIFE
BOOKS

Other Publications:
THE TIME-LIFE COMPLETE GARDENER
THE NEW HOME REPAIR AND IMPROVEMENT
JOURNEY THROUGH THE MIND AND BODY
WEIGHT WATCHERS® SMART CHOICE RECIPE COLLECTION
TRUE CRIME
THE ART OF WOODWORKING
LOST CIVILIZATIONS
ECHOES OF GLORY
THE NEW FACE OF WAR
HOW THINGS WORK
WINGS OF WAR
CREATIVE EVERYDAY COOKING
COLLECTOR'S LIBRARY OF THE UNKNOWN
CLASSICS OF WORLD WAR II
TIME-LIFE LIBRARY OF CURIOUS AND UNUSUAL FACTS
AMERICAN COUNTRY
VOYAGE THROUGH THE UNIVERSE
THE THIRD REICH
MYSTERIES OF THE UNKNOWN
TIME FRAME
FIX IT YOURSELF
FITNESS, HEALTH & NUTRITION
SUCCESSFUL PARENTING
HEALTHY HOME COOKING
UNDERSTANDING COMPUTERS
LIBRARY OF NATIONS
THE ENCHANTED WORLD
THE KODAK LIBRARY OF CREATIVE PHOTOGRAPHY
GREAT MEALS IN MINUTES
THE CIVIL WAR
PLANET EARTH
COLLECTOR'S LIBRARY OF THE CIVIL WAR
THE EPIC OF FLIGHT
THE GOOD COOK
WORLD WAR II
THE OLD WEST

For information on and a full description of any of the Time-Life Books series listed above, please call 1-800-621-7026 or write:
Reader Information
Time-Life Customer Service
P.O. Box C-32068
Richmond, Virginia 23261-2068

This volume is one of a series that chronicles the history and culture of the Native Americans. Other books in the series include:

The Cover: Wearing traditional beadwork clothing handed down through her family, Carla HighEagle, a Nez Percé, stands before the tall grass and rolling hills of her northwest Idaho homeland. HighEagle is active in several tribal groups aimed at enhancing cultural awareness, including the First Horse Program, which teaches reservation children the equestrian skills for which their ancestors were famous.

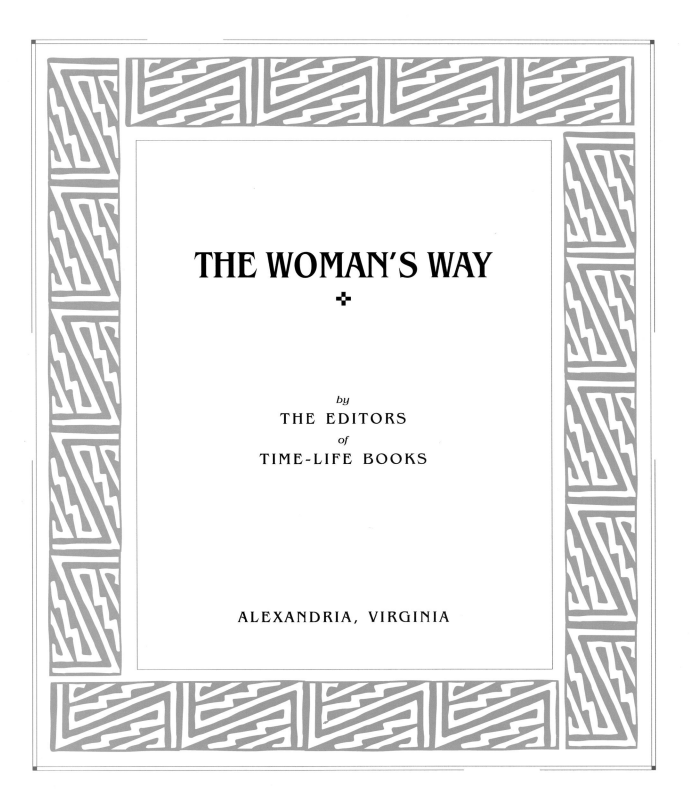

THE WOMAN'S WAY

✤

by
THE EDITORS
of
TIME-LIFE BOOKS

ALEXANDRIA, VIRGINIA

Time-Life Books is a division of Time Life Inc.

PRESIDENT and CEO: John M. Fahey Jr.
EDITOR-IN-CHIEF: John L. Papanek

TIME-LIFE BOOKS

MANAGING EDITOR: Roberta Conlan

Director of Design: Michael Hentges
Director of Editorial Operations: Ellen Robling
Director of Photography and Research: John Conrad Weiser
Senior Editors: Russell B. Adams Jr., Dale M. Brown, Janet Cave, Lee Hassig, Robert Somerville, Henry Woodhead
Special Projects Editor: Rita Thievon Mullin
Director of Technology: Eileen Bradley
Library: Louise D. Forstall

PRESIDENT: John D. Hall

Vice President, Director of Marketing: Nancy K. Jones
Vice President, New Product Development:
Neil Kagan
Vice President, Book Production: Marjann Caldwell
Production Manager: Marlene Zack
Quality Assurance Manager: Miriam P. Newton

THE AMERICAN INDIANS

SERIES EDITOR: Henry Woodhead
Administrative Editor: Loretta Y. Britten

Editorial Staff for *The Woman's Way*
Senior Art Director: Ray Ripper
Picture Editor: Susie Kelly
Text Editor: John Newton (principal), Stephen G. Hyslop
Associate Editors/Research-Writing: Mary Helena McCarthy (principal), Trudy W. Pearson, Jennifer Veech
Senior Copyeditor: Ann Lee Bruen
Picture Coordinator: Daryl Beard
Editorial Assistant: Christine Higgins

Special Contributors: Amy Aldrich, Maggie Debelius, Marfé Ferguson Delano, Michelle Murphy, Susan Perry, Lydia Preston, David S. Thomson, Gerald P. Tyson (text); Martha Lee Beckington, Barbara Fleming, Debra Diamond Smit, Veronica Torres, Anne Whittle (research); Barbara L. Klein (index).

Correspondents: Christine Hinze (London), Christina Lieberman (New York), Maria Vincenza Aloisi (Paris), Ann Natanson (Rome). Valuable assistance was also provided by: Barbara Gevene Hertz (Copenhagen), Elizabeth Brown (New York), Carolyn Sackett (Seattle).

Library of Congress Cataloging in Publication Data
The woman's way/by the editors of Time-Life Books.
p. cm.—(The American Indians)
Includes bibliographical references and index.
ISBN 0-8094-9729-8
1. Indian women—North America—History
2. Indian women—North America—Social life and customs. I. Time-Life Books. II. Series.
E98.W8W65 1995   94-38432
305.48'897—dc20   CIP

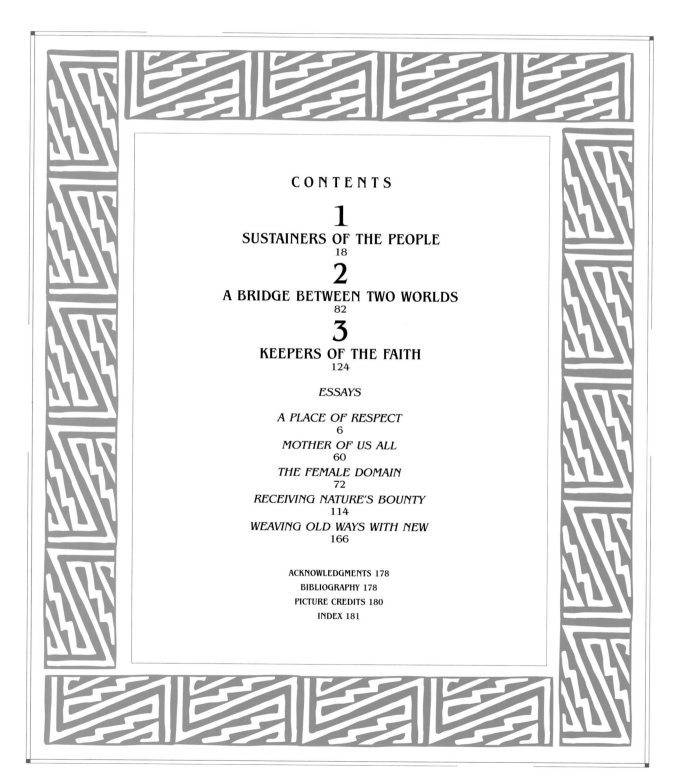

CONTENTS

1
SUSTAINERS OF THE PEOPLE

2
A BRIDGE BETWEEN TWO WORLDS

3
KEEPERS OF THE FAITH

ESSAYS

A PLACE OF RESPECT

Through the ages, Indian women have occupied positions of honor in their tribes. Although their exact status depended on the economic and social structures of their communities, Indian women have long been revered as the mothers of the people, responsible for feeding, clothing, and sheltering the generations. They have also earned respect in other areas—from healing and religion to economics and policymaking, sometimes even as warriors. In many cultures, they controlled the fundamental institutions of society, including the rights to clan membership, tribal leadership, and the use of tribal lands. These portraits reflect that proud and ancient heritage.

NEZ PERCE BABY

CHEYENNE GIRLS

KWAKIUTL ADOLESCENT

HOPI ADOLESCENT

INUIT YOUNG WOMAN

APACHE YOUNG WOMEN

OSAGE MOTHER AND CHILD

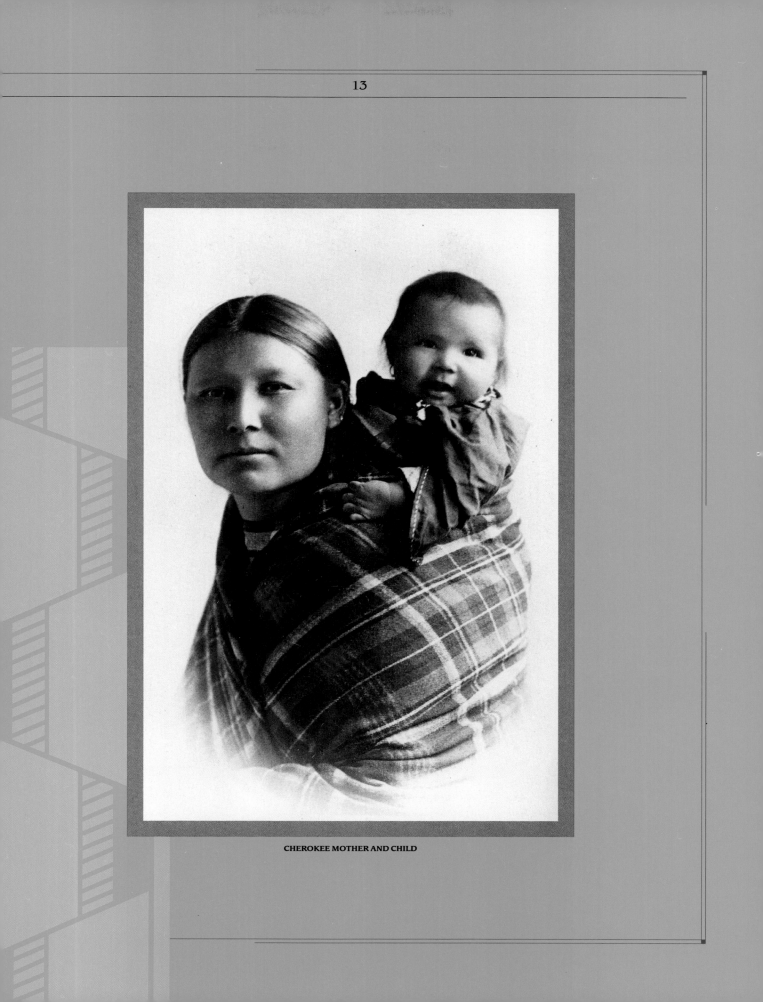

CHEROKEE MOTHER AND CHILD

COMANCHE WOMAN

POMO WOMAN

HUPA FEMALE ELDERS

ELDERLY COAST SALISH WOMAN

1

SUSTAINERS OF THE PEOPLE

Watching from afar, Sioux women lend their support to the Sun Dance, an annual ritual vital to the preservation of their people, in this drawing by a Sioux artist. Often anonymous to outsiders, Indian women—symbolized above by vulva-shaped rock carvings from the Pacific Northwest—have always occupied positions of respect within their communities.

The events that cast a young Indian girl as the heroine of one of the most enduring legends in American history allegedly occurred on a cold December day in the year 1607. A pale frost coated the bare corn and bean fields surrounding the village of Werowocomoco, situated several miles up the York River from the lower Chesapeake Bay. The settlement was the capital of a powerful confederacy of Algonquian-speaking Indians whose collective lands encompassed the Tidewater region of present-day Virginia.

The werowance, or principal chief, of the confederacy sat wrapped in raccoon skins on a broad throne inside his longhouse. Although his proper name was Wahunsonacock, he was known as Powhatan, or Falls in a Current, after the name of one of his favorite residences located at a site opposite the James River rapids near the modern city of Richmond. Ropes of pearls hung from his neck, glimmering in the dim light of the hearth fires. Thick smoke filled the air. Around Powhatan stood his wives and counselors and more than 200 of his people. The slight figure of his favorite daughter, Matoaka, affectionately called Pocahontas—or Playful One—was all but lost in the crowd.

At a signal from Powhatan, two large flat stones were placed on the ground in front of the assembly. Several warriors dragged an English soldier to the crude altar and shoved his face against its hard surface. The captive, 28-year-old Captain John Smith, who was leader of the tiny English colony at Jamestown, seemingly had only moments to live. Stone clubs were poised to crush his skull, when suddenly Pocahontas ran from her father's side. She threw herself across Smith's body and laid her head over the Englishman's own, sending her long black hair cascading over his face. "Whereat," Smith subsequently wrote in a third-person account of the event, "the Emperor was contented he should live."

Published in 1624 in his *Generall Historie of Virginia,* John Smith's dramatic retelling of his rescue from a cruel and ignominious death by a beautiful Indian "princess" enthralled the English public. From the time of Columbus, European artists had employed the fanciful figure of a bare-

breasted Indian woman as an allegorical symbol for the New World. The Pocahontas story complemented this image. Yet even at the time, some of John Smith's contemporaries questioned whether the events at Werowocomoco actually took place. The only account of them was the ambitious adventurer's own florid narrative. Its implication that the chief's daughter—who was probably little more than 12 years old at the time—was moved to her heroic act because she was smitten with him was highly improbable. Critics still scoff at the notion, along with the far-fetched suggestion that Pocahontas—whose marriage to John Rolfe in 1614 brought about a brief truce between the Indians and the Jamestown settlers—was motivated by nascent Christian sensibilities.

In light of what is now known about 17th-century coastal Algonquian society, modern scholars have another explanation for the Pocahontas story. It does not dispute the central facts as John Smith told them, but offers a far different interpretation. In 1607 Powhatan was under considerable pressure from members of his confederacy to annihilate the settlers. But the chief himself favored forming an alliance with them. It appears likely that Powhatan, in keeping with the Algonquian practice of adopting enemy captives, decided to take the English leader into his family in order to forge a bond with the whites. He used his favorite daughter as the ceremonial instrument to enact his policy. As a high-ranking female, Pocahontas served as a mother figure for Smith's rebirth as an Indian after he first

This fanciful 19th-century engraving of a bare-breasted Pocahontas rescuing Captain John Smith from her "barbarous" relatives is but one of many illustrations of the apocryphal event that introduced a popular stereotype of the Indian woman.

underwent a symbolic death through mock execution. Her intercession was not the impulsive act of a tender-hearted girl but part of a ritual that neither Smith nor his compatriots understood.

Today, nearly 400 years after John Smith's famous "rescue," a host of misconceptions still envelop Native American women. From the first, most European observers viewed the Indians through the distorting prism of their own vastly different culture and were often blind not only to the distinctive patterns of interaction between Indian men and women but also to the social influence that shaped their lives.

Father Paul Le Jeune, superior of the Jesuit mission that was established at Quebec in the 1630s, gave a typical account of women's responsibilities among the bands of Montagnais and Naskapi living in the upper Saint Lawrence River valley of northeastern Canada. "The women," he wrote, "besides the onerous role of rearing the children, also transport the game from the place where it has fallen; they are the hewers of wood and drawers of water; they make and repair the household utensils; they prepare food; they skin the game and prepare the hides like fullers; they sew garments; they catch fish and gather shellfish for food; often they even hunt; they make the canoes, that is skiffs of marvelous rapidity, out of bark; they set up the tents wherever and whenever they stop for the night—in short, the men concern themselves with nothing but the more laborious hunting and the waging of war."

And yet from the Indian perspective, this division of labor between males and females was the natural order of things—and a necessity for survival in their environment. Social tradition dictated that both sexes have clearly defined roles in separate but complementary spheres. Throughout the Indian world, women functioned much as Father Le Jeune described—bearing, tending, and educating the children, processing and cooking the food, making the clothing and other domestic articles. Although the Montagnais and Naskapi lived too far north to grow crops, agriculture was also part of the woman's sphere. Even among the Pueblo peoples of the Southwest, where the men did the majority of the farming, women were considered the owners of the harvests.

Manhood, on the other hand, was largely defined by hunting and warfare—especially in the warrior-centered societies of the Plains, the prairies, and the East. In some areas, tribes lived in danger of attack from rival groups, and a man's chief responsibility was to remain constantly ready to defend the women and children. Hunting required similar vigilance, for the men had to keep up with game and also maintain the readiness of

Je, a 72-year-old Cherokee midwife, radiates quiet dignity in this 1920s photograph. Indian midwives enjoyed great esteem for their role in ushering in new generations.

their equipment. "They had to be in shape to fight at any time, day or night," explained a 19th-century Crow woman named Pretty Shield of her people's warriors. "War, killing meat and bringing it into camp, horse stealing and taking care of horses, gave our men plenty of work."

Most Indian groups tolerated exceptions to the general rules that established the roles of men and women, however. Females could take on the responsibilities of men if they wished and vice versa. Thus, on occasion, Indian women served as hunters, scouts, diplomats, and even warriors. Most Europeans neither perceived nor understood such flexibility. The image of the degraded and lowly "squaw"—the term being a corruption of the Narragansett word for woman—became as vivid a stereotype of Indian womanhood as the noble princess personified by Pocahontas. Such inaccurate images have persistently obscured the contributions made by the original female occupants of North America. Much of their rich history has been lost forever. The early European observers were principally interested in the military, trading, and diplomatic exploits of Indian men and gave only cursory and often imprecise attention to the homely domestic lives of the women and their roles as mothers, daughters, wives, and grandmothers, to say nothing of their skills as gardeners, traders, artisans, and healers.

In all tribes, women were valued for their labors. "They were esteemed the mistresses of the soil," stated a sachem of the Oneida, one of the original Five Nations of the Iroquois, in 1788. "Who bring us into being? Who cultivate our lands, kindle our fires, and boil our pots but the women?" In some tribes, women contributed as much as 80 percent of the labor needed to produce the family food supply—not only raising, gathering, and preparing the plants that were the traditional female domain but also butchering, storing, and cooking the meat brought in by the men. They were treasured as well for their roles as healers and midwives, and for their skills in crafting material goods, from ceremonial and trade objects to boats and shelters. The Navajo hogan, the Apache wickiup, and the tipis of the Great Plains tribes were designed and constructed by women.

Following a time-honored custom, a Navajo woman in a modern hospital pulls on a hand-woven sash during childbirth. Traditionally, Navajo women tied a sash to a tree to hold on to during labor.

Beadwork adorns this turtle-shaped pouch, made to hold the umbilical cord of a Plains Indian baby girl. (Pouches for boys resembled lizards or snakes.) The amulets were carried or worn to ensure good health and longevity.

Across North America, women were revered as the central life-giving force. In the stories that many Indians told to explain their origins, it was female powers who created the earth itself. And the very key to every tribe's continued existence was its women's ability to bring forth and nurture future generations. "It is well to be good to women in the strength of our manhood," a Sioux elder once observed, "because we must sit under their hands at both ends of our lives."

Early Europeans who took the care to closely observe Indian life were surprised at the degree of autonomy enjoyed by Indian women. Typically, a married Indian woman retained control of all the goods she possessed before her marriage or produced during it. A man could not appropriate his wife's possessions. Nor could he control her reproductive rights. Women spaced their pregnancies widely. They generally could not be forced to marry against their will and could easily dissolve their marriages if they chose to do so. Father Le Jeune tried vainly to introduce the Montagnais to the European family structure, with its presumption of male authority. He often lectured that in France the man was "the master." But among the Indians, the opposite seemed to be true. To the Jesuit's great frustration, Montagnais women made all the important decisions regarding the choice "of plans, of undertakings, of journeys, of winterings." Still, the priest marveled at the harmonious relationships Montagnais husbands and wives enjoyed. It derived, he concluded, from the division of labor. The women "know what they are to do, and the men also; and one never meddles with the work of the other."

Despite widely different environments and social systems, the rearing of little girls remained remarkably similar in every Native American culture. As parents, Indians were permissive, and the bond between mothers and daughters was close. "They are very often accompanied by their daughters," wrote the Englishman Thomas Hariot in 1585, noting the affectionate relationships between Indian mothers and their little girls living in the coastal villages of what is today North Carolina.

A young girl's education began early, as the growing youngster observed and gradually participated in the myriad domestic tasks that women of her society performed. Every juvenile effort was celebrated. In Salish villages of the coastal Northwest, the baskets, bags, and beadwork made by little girls were draped over the bushes along the footpaths to be admired by passersby. Mesquakie girls, living in what is now Wisconsin

and Illinois, were given seeds to plant and then lavished with praise when they cooked meals from the produce they had grown. "The first pair of moccasins I made were for my father," recalled an elderly Cheyenne woman, reminiscing in 1931 about her childhood. "My mother would show me how to twist the sinews, and how to cut the soles and uppers for different sizes." Her father's praise so encouraged the little girl that she began employing her budding skills to make footwear for the other children in her camp. She also joined her girlfriends in games of make-believe that imitated the ways and customs of grownups. "Our mothers made rag dolls of women, boys, girls, and babies," she recalled. "We used forked sticks to represent ponies, and we mounted the people on the fork of the sticks, pretending to move camp. Sometimes a baby would be born; or a marriage would take place—in fact anything that we knew about older people."

Indian girls were also encouraged to be physically active. Not only did exercise promote grace and beauty, it also built strength for childbearing and strenuous work. Among the Lakota Sioux and some other Plains peo-

A little Kiowa girl wearing a buckskin dress is honored during her first dance. Traditionally, a family celebrates the event—which marks the child's entrance into a new aspect of community life—by bestowing gifts on friends.

A five-year-old Navajo girl works at a traditional Navajo loom. Weaving remains a critical skill in Navajo society, and young girls are instructed in it from an early age.

Photographed in the 1890s, a Kiowa toddler poses with her doll and miniature cradleboard. Native American girls often played with toys that helped them learn to be good mothers.

ples, boys and girls were separated at an early age and schooled in different behavior—including even separate male and female patterns of speech and the manner of sitting on the ground. But in most Indian communities, boys and girls mixed freely. Young girls from the coastal areas of the Northeast, for example, led active, unconfined lives, joining their male companions in spirited ball games, diving for mussels in the offshore waters, catching frogs and terrapins, and stalking small game in the forests.

Delfina Cuero, a Kumeyaay Indian from southern California, has described growing up in the early 1900s. When Cuero was not helping her mother gather wild plants for food, she was roughhousing with playmates of both sexes. "We used to have wars against the boys," she recalled of a game in which the children threw gourds at each other. "Sometimes boys and girls would be on both teams, and other times it would be boys against girls." Cuero also ran footraces, hunted rabbits, and jumped off high rocks to prove her bravery.

In quieter moments, Indian girls learned the manners and mores of their people. Storytelling was the favored means of instruction. Every Indian mother had an ample stock of cautionary tales to impart useful truths. "We knew that these stories were told to teach us how to behave and what to expect," recalled Cuero, who was particularly impressed by a tale about a male coyote and two beautiful crow sisters. The coyote constantly begged the crows to take him flying. Eventually the younger crow fell under his spell. Despite her sister's warnings, she threw down a rope from her perch—allowing the coyote to ascend high enough to grab her. She was saved in the nick of time by her older sister, who cut the rope and sent the coyote plummeting to his death. "This story explains how we have to watch men," concluded Cuero.

The instructions on proper conduct and physical conditioning intensified as a girl approached puberty. Mourning Dove, a Salish woman who grew up in Washington State at the turn of the 20th century, remembered how difficult it was for her to accept the increasing demands her mother and grandmother placed on her. "I was made to run uphill without stopping until I reached the top of each of the little round knolls close to our home," she recalled. "This was intended to strengthen my lungs and increase my wind power. I had to carry all the water in the house. If I stopped to pout, I was ordered to run rather than walk to the spring. This was to give me energy for my lifework. Deep in my heart, I felt that my parents were being most cruel to me. Their pampering had suddenly stopped."

The true end of childhood was signaled by menarche, a girl's first menstrual period. The beginning of the menstrual function was universally regarded as a major event, both in the life of the individual and in the community at large; it was the sign that a female had reached womanhood and was capable of bearing children for her people. But the mysterious power of the menarche also brought inherent dangers. All Indian peoples believed that menstrual blood was a potent force, akin to the power ascribed to warriors who have followed the proper rituals before heading into combat. Whereas the warrior is prepared to take life, the menstruating female is in a position to give life. Both powers were deemed ambivalent—capable of conferring either benefits or afflictions.

In a custom that was observed by many cultures, an Indian woman spends her menstrual period in a segregated hut. Menstruating women were thought to be at the height of their medicine; men who came in contact with them risked losing certain powers.

"When a girl is young, she is like a boy," a Lakota man once explained, "but when she has her first menstrual flow, a *tonwan* (spirit) possesses her, which gives her the possibility of motherhood and makes her *wakan* (powerful), and this tonwan is in the products of her first menstrual flow, making it powerful for good or evil."

Like many other Native Americans, the Lakota people traditionally believed that the spirit of menstruation was inimical to the male. They characterized its effect as *ohakaya,* a concept that translates roughly as "cause to be blocked or tangled." The power of a menstruating girl was considered to be so great that it could even weaken the power of a medicine man. Any man who came near a girl menstruating for the first time, it was believed, was likely to be plagued thereafter with tremors or madness. To guard against such danger, a Lakota girl at menarche was required to sit over a hole dug an arm's length into the ground so that her blood would mingle with the more compatible powers of the earth.

Nearly every tribe observed certain taboos to channel the menstrual power. Some of them were aimed at the girl; it was widely believed in some cultures, for example, that her future success as a woman hung on the correct observance of such strictures as drinking water only through a reed, eating with separate utensils, and avoiding scratching herself with her fingernails. Other taboos protected the community, particularly aspects of life having to do with men. A menstruating woman could not come near a medicine bundle, or touch a hunting implement or a weapon, lest she ruin the sights of a gun, make a pony go lame, cause arrows to miss their mark, or affect a hunter's eyesight.

Just as a warrior returning from combat was not allowed to enter his village or have sexual intercourse until he had undergone a period of ritu-

In some Northwest tribes, menstruating women used special medicine kits like the one below. Its contents—rotten wood, fungus, and mineral-rich chunks of earth—were used to regulate a woman's monthly cycle.

Drinking tubes, such as these made from bird bones, were used by menstruating women in the Pacific Northwest to prevent water from touching their lips. Many Native American cultures observed similar taboos.

al purification, so a woman was segregated from the rest of the community at the onset of each period. In some cultures, she stayed in her own home in a specially partitioned area. In others, she was secluded in a small hut—in many cases, in a remote location. Ojibwa girls who retired to brush structures deep in the forests scattered leaves behind themselves to warn men, pregnant women, and women with small babies to keep away. The Yurok women of northwestern California considered the menstrual blood a purifying as well as powerful force and looked upon the menstrual seclusion as a time to acquire fresh spiritual energy.

A girl's first stay in menstrual confinement was often accompanied by special initiation rites appropriate to the occasion. A Kumeyaay girl, for example, had to remain in a sand-filled pit for four days, while the older women danced around her, singing. Some of the songs were about food in order to test her ability to withstand hunger; others were instructional. "Nobody just talked about these things ever," recalled Delfina Cuero. "It was all in the songs and myths that belonged to the ceremony. All that a girl needed to know to be a good wife, and how to have babies and to take care of them, was learned at the ceremony at the time when a girl became a woman."

In the Pacific Northwest, Tlingit girls experiencing their first menses were kept in a dark room for a period of time, the length of which depended on their families' status. A girl from a very high ranking family could be confined for as long as two years. She wore a hood hung with heavy tassels of dentalium shells to prevent her looking upward for fear that her gaze would bring storms or other natural disasters. Her father's sister or sometimes her mother or maternal grandmother cared for her and taught her the traditions of her womenfolk. The girl emerged from her confinement with a pale complexion and legs so shaky she could barely walk— signs to be envied because they attested to her family's high rank.

Not surprisingly, some Indian girls feared the onset of menses. Having been told that even a fleeting glance from a menstruating woman would contaminate a man's blood, a Winnebago girl named Mountain Wolf Woman, born in the late 1800s, fled weeping into the Wisconsin woods on the winter morning when her first period began. "The snow was still on the ground and the trees were just beginning to bud," she recalled. "In the woods there was a broken tree and I sat down under this fallen tree. I bowed my head with my blanket wrapped over me and there I was, crying

To attract the man of her choice, an Ojibwa girl sang special songs or hired a medicine woman (left) to sing on her behalf. Manido-gicigo-kwe, the woman in this early-20th-century photograph, also sold love charms and special powders to kindle romance.

and crying." Mountain Wolf Woman kept her head under the blanket until her sister and sister-in-law found her by following her footprints in the snow. They built her a little canvas-covered wigwam, and there she sat, hungry and alone, for the next four days.

The Salish woman Mourning Dove was out riding when her first period started. "I sat down on a big boulder and cried," she recalled. Then she walked slowly home, leading her beloved pony and trying to delay the moment he would be taken away from her, because according to Salish belief, the touch of a menstruating woman might cause a horse's hair to fall out. "I was lingering purposely to be alone in my sorrow," she wrote. "I was then just 12 years old. Up to this time I had played with other children and boys. I loved my freedom."

When an Indian girl reappeared after her first menstrual confinement, she was officially a woman. Generally there was some public acknowledgment that this critical passage had occurred. Some groups—most notably the Navajo and Apache—staged elaborate ceremonies lasting for days and featuring feasts for a multitude of guests. A Cheyenne father publicly announced his daughter's first menses from the tipi door and marked the occasion by giving away a horse; a Tlingit father gave a potlatch. In other cultures, families celebrated with private rituals. Kumeyaay elders tattooed a girl around the mouth and chin. Salish mothers tied what was known as a virgin cape over the shoulders of their daughters to shield their bodies from male eyes.

In many cultures, the menarche was soon followed by marriage. Adult womanhood was synonymous with matrimony. An Indian spinster, like an unmarried man, was an anomaly, outside the natural order and at odds with a society in which the two sexes depended on each other for survival.

Some tribes allowed young women a few years to perfect their domestic skills. But in other groups—those that put a premium on chastity—girls were married quickly to ensure they would wed as virgins. Girls in these cultures had few opportunities to meet young men prior to marriage, and their mothers often deliberately instilled a fear of the opposite sex, hoping that their daughters would be too timid to allow men to approach them. A Tohono O'odham, or Papago, girl, for example, was taught that if she daydreamed about a particular boy, a snake would disguise himself as the boy and make love to her. The Kootenay of southeastern British Columbia and the American Northwest warned their girls that illicit sex would turn them into frogs at some point in the afterlife.

Among the Plains tribes, unchaste girls risked public disgrace. As a result, families chaperoned their daughters closely. Men who managed to seduce young women sometimes treated their conquests as coups—boasting about their exploits in songs that mentioned the girls by name. The Apache also put great stock in virginity. An unmarried Apache girl who was discovered to have had sexual relations was sometimes publicly whipped by her father as an object lesson to other young women.

Other Indian cultures considered premarital sex a natural part of life. Among some Pueblo groups, couples intending to marry were expected to sleep together. The Pueblos also tended to take illegitimacy in stride; instead of stigmatizing an unmarried mother, they supported her in the same way that they supported widows with young children.

Similar sexual freedom prevailed among many eastern tribes. Unmarried Natchez women living along the lower Mississippi River, for example, competed with one another to see who could attract the most men and receive the most presents from them. Large numbers of gifts from former lovers testified to a Natchez woman's desirability and made up a large part of her dowry. Among some groups within the Iroquois League, young women experimented freely with sex, testing out lovers and entering into trial marriages. An Iroquois man who wished to marry first asked permission from the girl's parents. He then gave the young woman a wampum necklace, bracelet, or a pair of earrings. If she was interested, she slept with her suitor for three or four nights on a trial basis. The Huron, or Wyandot, also believed in multiple companionships, legitimizing a union only when a child was conceived.

A young woman's marriage was usually arranged by her family. In general, girls had the right to refuse their parents' choice, but few of them did so. Marriage was not expected to be a love match—rather, it was viewed as a social contract for sharing economic responsibilities and child rearing. To ensure their material well-being, young women were frequently married to older men. They did not expect to have emotionally intimate relationships with their husbands, but rather with the children they bore, their blood relations or clans, and the other women of the community. If they were incompatible with their husbands, most Indian women could easily divorce. An English trader writing about the 18th-century Cherokee noted, "I have seen them leave one the other in eight or 10 days with as little concern as if they never had known one another." It was not uncommon for Ojibwa and Cree women to marry seven or eight times. When the Winnebago girl Mountain Wolf Woman was being pressured into marrying a man who had done her brother a favor, her mother consoled her by saying, "When you are older and know better, you can marry whoever you want to marry."

In most cultures, a woman who was living with her husband's family separated from him by simply gathering up her belongings and small children and returning home to her parents. If, on the other hand, the couple was living with the wife's family or in a dwelling that was her property—as was common in many tribes—she just put the man's belongings outside and told him to leave. Among the Nomlaki of northern California, the woman signaled her desire to separate by weaving a basket, pouting as she worked. When the basket was finished, she handed it to her husband and announced her decision to leave.

The casualness of Indian divorce and the ease with which people accepted new partners shocked the Christian missionaries who were sent to work among the Native Americans. Complaining that he could not baptize potential converts if they persisted in divorcing a disagreeable wife or husband, Father Le Jeune said of the Montagnais and Naskapi: "The young people do not think that they can persevere in the state of matrimony with

This 1877 drawing by a Kiowa named Wohaw illustrates a Plains courting ritual, in which a man formally signaled his interest in a woman by enveloping her in his blanket for quiet conversation. Women were free to accept or refuse the invitation.

a bad wife or a bad husband. Since I have been preaching among them that a man should not have more than one wife, I have not been well received by the women; for, since they are more numerous than the men, if a man can only marry one of them, the others will have to suffer."

Two dominant factors shaped the life of a Native American woman: her people's means of subsistence and their kinship system. The first set the pattern of her daily existence; the second provided the framework that determined her status. For the most part, women who lived in cultures where kinship was reckoned matrilineally, that is, through the female line, and whose people subsisted principally on the products of female agriculture wielded the greatest influence. Such was the situation that generally prevailed among the Indians living east of the Mississippi River. Most of these peoples—including the Seneca, Cayuga, Mohawk, Onondaga, and Oneida of the Iroquois League, the mid-Atlantic coastal Algonquian tribes, and the peoples of the southern woodlands, such as the Cherokee, Chickasaw, Creek, and Natchez—dwelt in permanent villages surrounded by cultivated fields of corn, squash, and beans. Descent was traced through the fe-

A Kwakiutl bride displays her wedding clothes in this 1890s photograph. Through marriage, a Kwakiutl woman transmitted her father's crests and ceremonial privileges to her husband.

male line and residence was commonly matrilocal, meaning that married couples resided with the wives' families.

Prior to the arrival of the Europeans, the original five Iroquois nations—whose territory stretched across what is now New York State—and the Huron, their neighbors and traditional enemies to the north, lived in communities of longhouses, each of which was occupied by a close-knit group of related females along with their children and spouses. Each maternal lineage group—known as an *ohwachira*—collectively owned the longhouse and its furnishings as well as the household's major economic resources, fields, and tools. This property was passed down from the older women to their daughters. In addition, each ohwachira was in control of the family burial grounds, the seeds for planting, and the stocks of wampum and dried food that constituted the public treasury.

A Coyotero Apache couple pose for a portrait about 1888. Apache marriages required the blessing of the elder relatives as well as the giving of proper gifts by the family of the groom to the family of the bride.

Marriage, which was arranged by the ohwachira, did not change a woman's residence or her status. In the event of a divorce, the husband left the household and any children; their support was solely the responsibility of the maternal line.

Iroquois men, who spent a good part of the year away from home on hunting, fighting, or trading expeditions, occupied a marginal position in these female-centered households. They were expected to help the women clear the fields and to provide meat, but otherwise had little to say about domestic affairs.

Iroquois social and ceremonial life centered on agriculture. The annual cycle of rituals was largely the province of three female societies: the Sisters of the Three Life Sustainers, who performed fertility ceremonies to promote the growth of crops; the Society of the Women Planters, who held the Green Corn Ceremony at harvesttime; and the Sisters of the Life Supporters, who conducted the planting ceremonies. The Iroquois believed that the soil would not bear fruit unless it was cultivated by women. The female power of fertility was deemed necessary in order for crops to grow; it was also thought that a woman could enrich the soil merely by walking around the fields, dragging her garments over the ground.

In each Iroquois village, agricultural production was controlled by an organized group of women who worked together. Grandmothers and aunts cared for the children, while the more physically active younger women carried out the gardening tasks. Time lost by one woman through childbirth or illness was made up by other members of her group.

Mary Jemison, an English colonist captured at the age of 15 in 1758 during the

French and Indian War, was adopted by the Seneca, one of the original Five Nations of the Iroquois. She lived with them for 65 years, during which time she married and raised five children. Jemison described the agricultural work as one of harmonious cooperation. "In order to expedite their business and at the same time enjoy each other's company, they all work together in one field or at whatever job they may have on hand," she explained. Each spring, the village elected a respected older woman as head field matron. The matron's job was to coordinate the work of planting, hoeing, harvesting, and storing the crops, which included more than 15 types of corn and as many as 60 varieties of beans, squash, potatoes, nuts, and peppers. Seeds were soaked for days to hasten germination, and tender plants such as squash sometimes started inside the longhouses in bark trays filled with a rich soil of powdered wood.

It was customary for Seneca women to work their fields in orchestrated succession, each woman planting a single row in each field. "They then go into the next field and plant one across, and so on until the whole is finished," Jemison explained. "By this rule, they perform their labor of every kind and every jealousy of one having done more or less than another is effectually avoided." The field matron mediated disputes and supervised the rest periods when the women amused each other by singing, playing games, and telling stories.

The close relationships that were forged by the women's working the fields together, coupled with the prolonged absences of the men, strengthened the power of the Iroquois matrons. In every Iroquois community, a Council of Clan Mothers, consisting of the heads of each household, was responsible for nominating men of their lineage as the sachems, or chiefs, who sat on the Grand Council of the league. In addition, the women helped set the agenda of league meetings and lobbied to influence votes. Their control of food supplies gave them a virtual veto over major decisions, including even the decision to go to war. They also controlled the fate of prisoners brought back by the warriors. Frequently, the women chose to adopt the captives to replace their kinsmen who had been killed in battle. But if a woman demanded revenge, the war chiefs were obliged to comply, and the victim died a slow death by ritual torture—even if the woman's wishes conflicted with tribal policy.

In 1654 a female member of the Erie, a small Iroquoian-speaking tribe, demanded that a captured Onondaga sachem be killed as compensation for her slain brother. The Erie sachems pleaded with her to spare the prominent captive, pointing out that the more populous and powerful

An Osage bride wears a U.S. military jacket and epaulets as part of her wedding costume. A peace medal hangs around her neck as a decoration.

Onondaga would be sure to exact terrible revenge if he was harmed. But the grieving woman insisted that he die, and her people had no choice but to oblige, setting off a war that ultimately destroyed the Erie.

"There is nothing more real than this superiority of the women," the Jesuit missionary Joseph-François Lafitau wrote of the Iroquois in 1724. "It is of them that the nation really consists, and it is through them that the nobility of the blood, the genealogical tree, and the families are perpetuated. All real authority is vested in them. The land, the fields, and their harvest all belong to them. They are the souls of the councils, the arbiters of peace and of war. They have charge of the public treasury. To them are given the slaves. They arrange marriages. The children are their domain, and it is through their blood that the order of succession is transmitted. The men, on the other hand, are entirely isolated."

Although the sweeping authority of Iroquois women was unparalleled, women in other matrilineal eastern tribes also had well-established paths to influence. Among the Algonquian-speaking groups—including the Narragansett of present-day Rhode Island, the Mohegan and Pequot of eastern Connecticut, the Montauk of Long Island, and the members of the Powhatan Confederacy—female shamans, or healers, wielded considerable power. Besides arranging marriages, high-ranking women also sponsored male political leaders and sometimes assumed formal leadership positions themselves. From 1656 until the mid-1680s, for example, the Pamunkey Indians were led by a descendant of Powhatan, a woman named Cockacoeske, whom the English called Queen Anne. Cockacoeske held the remnants of the old Powhatan Confederacy together for three decades. Under her leadership, the Pamunkey participated in a landmark peace agreement that governed relations with the English until the time of the Revolution. Cockacoeske was described by one colonist as an astute politician, "with grave courtlike gestures and a majestick air."

Indian women living on the central prairies and plains during the 18th and 19th centuries enjoyed less authority. More than 30 major tribes occupied that vast territory, stretching from Canada south into central Texas and from the Mississippi Valley west to the foothills of the Rocky Mountains. Some of these peoples were agriculturists who had migrated from the eastern woodlands to settle the rich flood plains of the region's rivers. Others were migratory hunters, following the great buffalo herds that furnished them with virtually every necessity.

Many prairie tribes lived for much of the year in earth-lodge villages, cultivating corn, squash, and sunflowers. They supplemented these crops with buffalo, deer, elk, and antelope meat taken during summer and winter hunts. In these groups, a woman's status was largely determined by the relative importance to the tribal economy of her agricultural products as opposed to the game supplied by the men.

The Mandan, a matrilineal tribe living on the upper Missouri River, subsisted mainly on agriculture. Corn was the dietary staple; game, normally hunted in short day trips, was less important. Consequently, women were the principal providers of food, and they enjoyed correspondingly high status. Mandan women owned the key economic resources—lodges, gardens, tools, and household goods. Two of the tribe's ritual societies were also the province of women. The Goose Society, which was devoted to ensuring good crops, was made up of women in their thirties and forties. The members held rainmaking ceremonies when drought threatened, and other ceremonies when the geese flew south in the fall and returned in the spring. In the winter, the White Buffalo Society—whose members were all women past menopause because it was believed that menstrual blood drove game away—performed buffalo-calling rites designed to lure the herds closer to the village. The White Buffalo Society extended Mandan women's influence into the male domain of hunting.

*Each of the seven clans of the Cherokee—
Wolf; Wild Potato, or Bear; Bird; Blue Pan-
ther, or Wildcat; Deer; Paint; and Wind,
or Long Hair—was represented by an honored woman who spoke for her clan, as
shown in this painting by Cherokee artist
Dorothy Tidwell Sullivan. The Beloved
Woman (holding a swan's wing) was their
spokeswoman. The Cherokee believed that
the Great Spirit spoke through her.*

An Assiniboin couple stand before their tipi. Plains Indian women were responsible for the construction and maintenance of their lodge—skills that enhanced their prestige in the tribe.

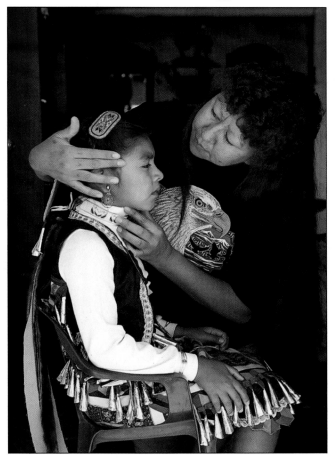

All dressed up for a powwow, a young Shoshone girl submits to her mother's last-minute inspection. Traditionally, an Indian woman's identity was linked to her family and home; as a result, she took pains to ensure that both reflected well on her.

Among the Pawnee of present-day Nebraska, male and female spheres were more rigidly defined. Like the Mandan, the Pawnee subsisted on both agriculture and hunting. But they depended more heavily on game than on crops, making men the principal providers and reducing the overall influence of women. Pawnee husbands generally lived with their wives' families only during the spring planting and fall harvest seasons. Then, communities lived in earth-lodge villages, with the women tending their fields and the men hunting local game. But in the summer and winter, when the Pawnee followed the buffalo and lived in tipis, the domestic situation was reversed. Households separated into smaller groups according to male kinship ties, and all activity revolved around the hunters and their needs.

With this greater reliance on game, the most important domestic alliance became the relationship between brothers. Groups of brothers hunted together and set up joint households during the buffalo season. Inheritance was governed by primogeniture; all property passed to a family's eldest son, who was responsible for the well-being of his siblings. The fact that men were the major heirs circumscribed women's lives. While Pawnee women owned their gardening plots and the tents they made, and controlled the distribution of food, they could not amass the economic resources and accompanying political influence possessed by women in more agriculturally intensive societies.

A similar situation prevailed on the Great Plains during the same time period. The lifestyle of buffalo-hunting tribes such as the Sioux, Cheyenne, and Comanche revolved around the male pursuits of warfare and hunting. Communities were organized around male kinship ties, and male warrior societies dominated tribal politics. The role of women was to support the hunters and warriors—a task that involved considerable labor. Women were responsible for all of the logistics involved with the nomadic life. "We were busy, especially when we were going to move," remembered the

Crow Indian Illustrations Drawn by Deaf Bull at Crow Agency M...

Crow woman Pretty Shield. Each time a group struck camp, it was the women who took down the tipis and packed the horses and travois; and at the next campsite, it was they who unpacked and pitched the tipis. This strenuous work was in addition to their regular domestic duties: gathering firewood and fetching water; cooking food, caring for children, and stitching up clothes, tipis, moccasins, and household utensils. Most important of all, the women processed the meat and hides that their husbands brought home from the hunt—a herculean task in the late fall when tribes were laying in stores for the winter.

During a successful fall hunting season, a single hunter killed an average of 50 buffalo. In order to prevent spoilage, each carcass had to be attended to immediately. The women scraped the still-warm hides clean of fat and tissue before the hides cooled and became too stiff to work. They cut up the meat and dried it into jerky or pounded it with an equal amount of fat to make a paste called pemmican. Each buffalo yielded about 45 pounds of dried meat and 55 pounds of pemmican. Then the women

This 1881 ledger drawing by a Crow named Deaf Bull may depict a man returning to a wife who had left him because he mistreated her. The woman's relatives are advising her what to do.

tanned each hide—a process that required from three to 10 days to complete, depending on what the hide was to be used for.

Although a skilled woman could butcher as many as three buffalo per day, even the most industrious could not keep up with all the work that needed to be done during the height of the hunting season. At the very least, it took the labor of two women to process the meat and hides of one hunter. As a consequence, every housewife had someone to help her—an elderly relative, a young girl, or, in those tribes that practiced polygamy, additional wives. An expert tanner was highly respected—so much so that among the Lakota the highest praise that a woman could receive was to be described as *slot'a,* meaning "full of grease." The term, which referred to a buckskin dress saturated with fat from the work of tanning hides and processing meat, symbolized the industry and skill that were regarded as among the most prized female virtues.

All Sioux groups valued women for their skill in crafting material goods. In much the same manner that the warriors kept count of war deeds, women tallied their domestic accomplishments—recording them in dots incised along the handles of the elk-horn tools that they employed for scraping hides. A black dot on one side represented one tanned robe; a red dot on the other side represented a tipi. Sioux women also held contests at which they exhibited and received prizes for their moccasins, dresses, storage bags, and cradleboards. Those who specialized in sewing and embellishing tipis, or the rawhide containers that were called parfleches by whites, discovered that their skills were a source of wealth. These women might be hired by others and paid in kind; a well-made cradleboard was as valuable as a horse.

The respect accorded a Plains Indian woman for her domestic skills reflected the premium that was placed on her work and the fact that men were the principal beneficiaries of her labor. A Blackfeet tale colorfully illustrates that point by describing a primeval world in which men and women lived apart from one another. The women were all well dressed and lived in handsome lodges, surrounded by beautiful possessions. The men were poor and homeless. Then each woman invited one man to live with her. Most of the men accepted. But the man chosen by the chief of the women rejected her because he found her too plain. For that he was turned into a pine tree, precariously rooted to the edge of a crumbling bank—just as any man so unwise as to spurn the loving attentions of a good woman was fated to teeter on the edge of oblivion.

The ideal of women's chastity and fidelity was cherished by Plains In-

THE IMPRINT OF BEAUTY

Although female beauty was valued in most Native American tribes, its definition—and the customs associated with it—varied widely from culture to culture. A sampling of different notions appears here and on the following pages.

dian society. It stood in sharp contrast to the license granted to men. Wives were expected to ignore their husbands' infidelities. But unfaithful women risked cruel retribution. Among some Sioux groups, a man had the right to punish an unfaithful wife by beating her or disfiguring her by cutting off the tip of her nose. In practice, however, men rarely employed such extreme measures, as they ran counter to the Plains Indian ideals of dignity and moderation. On the positive side, women were encouraged by the respect and esteem that faithfulness garnered. As a Sioux woman named Blue Whirlwind recalled, "A woman who had been married only once and been faithful was considered better than any other."

The supreme virtue of bravery was instilled in both sexes from earliest childhood. Although the highest prestige was accorded the warriors, Plains Indian women were as emotionally involved in warfare as the men, particularly during the decades of intense fighting in the 19th century. But they were largely barred from the glory attendant on counting coup, capturing enemy horses, and taking scalps. For the most part, their only outlet was to help their husbands or brothers by providing supplies, singing in ritual support of departing war parties, and imploring the warriors to avenge the deaths of loved ones.

Such socially sanctioned auxiliary activities were not enough to satisfy every woman. Some young wives turned their children over to grandmothers and accompanied their husbands on raids, helping out by prepar-

Two generations of Seris (left) display the intricate facial painting worn by the women of this tribe that lived on the desert coast of the Gulf of California in northwestern Mexico. The patterns signify family allegiance.

Red paint highlights the forehead, scalp, cheeks, and ears of Tissewoonatis, or She Who Bathes Her Knees, the wife of a Cheyenne chief, in this portrait painted by George Catlin in the 1830s.

ing food, nursing the wounded, and occasionally joining the fighting. A few defied tradition to become warriors in their own right.

In the early part of the 19th century, a little Gros Ventre girl was captured and raised by the Crow people. She grew up tall and strong, and her stepfather encouraged her to develop her aptitude for riding and shooting. Eventually she gained a reputation as a hunter, capable of killing five buffalo during a hunt—and then butchering them and loading them onto packhorses single-handedly. During her initial foray as a warrior, she killed one man and wounded two, so impressing her male companions that they composed songs in her honor. She was thereafter invited to join other war parties. Her skill at stealing horses won her a place in the Crow council of chiefs—and the name Woman Chief. In 1854 she was killed by a Gros Ventre warrior while she was attempting to negotiate a peace between the Crow and her former people.

A young Piegan Blackfeet called Brown Weasel Woman chose a similar male lifestyle. Like Woman Chief, she was taught by her father to shoot and ride like a boy. When her parents died, Brown Weasel Woman brought a widow into her lodge to tend house and care for her orphaned siblings. From then on, she acted as head of the family, carrying her father's rifle and going on raids with the warriors. While posted as a sentry during her first raid, she repulsed a number of Crows who had crept up to steal the Blackfeet ponies. Still, Brown Weasel Woman was not accepted by the

A Kwakiutl woman photographed about 1910 bears the elongated head that was once considered a mark of beauty by her people. Abandoned after her generation, the tradition of head flattening grew from a creation story in which the first man took a woman with a long head for a wife.

men. She was pressured to marry and settle down—to the degree that she finally sought an answer by going on a four-day solitary fast and quest for a vision. When she returned, she reported that the spirits had given her the power to lead war parties and that the Sun had appeared to her and told her that she must belong only to him and to no mortal man. Her path having been sanctified by this vision, Brown Weasel Woman was recognized as a warrior and honored with the name Running Eagle, a name carried by other famous Blackfeet warriors of the past. Running Eagle brought new luster to the name. She died in combat at the hands of a Salish warrior, probably in 1878.

The diverse tribes living in the arid lands south of the Great Plains met the challenges of their environment in a number of ways. The Pueblo peoples—among them the Zuni, the Hopi, and the Tewa—were for the most part sedentary agriculturists. They farmed the flood plains of the Rio Grande and its tributaries or planted in the arroyos and canyons dampened by the annual rains that ran off the high mesas where they built their apartment-like housing complexes.

The Athapaskan-speaking peoples of the North who entered the area about AD 1500 discovered ways in which they could live more directly off the land. Some bands, the ancestors of the Navajo, adopted agricultural

The process—and result—of head flattening is illustrated in this painting of a Cowlitz woman and her baby girl. A headboard tied to the foot of the cradleboard exerted continuous pressure on the infant's padded skull, causing her forehead to become elongated.

techniques from the Pueblos and acquired sheep and horses from the Spaniards. They became seminomadic pastoralists who wintered in sturdy structures called hogans and spent the warmer months moving to grasslands to graze their livestock.

Others, the forebears of the Apache, followed the movements of the region's game animals and the seasonal cycles of the plant life. Ranging from what is today western Oklahoma to eastern Arizona, and down through Texas and into Mexico, they eventually fragmented into six distinct tribes with similar cultures and subsistence patterns. For the most part, the Apache survived on the scattered bounty of desert and mountain, supplemented with provisions gained from raiding.

Whatever their means of subsistence, all southwestern peoples lived a precarious existence. The withering climate and fickle water supply were persistent reminders of the fragility of life. In consequence, many groups expressed their keen appreciation for fertility through a deep-seated respect for their women.

The Hopi acknowledged the central importance of childbearing in virtually every aspect of life—from the plethora of female symbols woven into ceremonies to promote bountiful crops to the economic advantages accorded women. Since there was little game in the Hopi's parched homeland, the men worked the corn, squash, and bean fields located in the bottom lands below their mesas. They were not, however, regarded as the

Dressed in beaded finery, a young Wishham woman from the Pacific Northwest is beautified by the tiny ring and a narrow piece of bone piercing her nose.

owners of these farmlands—the women were, just as the seeds for planting were considered the sacred property of each female-dominated household and passed down through the female line. Similarly, the crops grown and harvested by the men were turned over to the women—who were the sole owners of all agricultural products.

The Hopi women also owned their homes, all the household goods and furnishings, and the small gardens of chilies, onions, and herbs that they planted. Husbands lived with their wives' families and were expected to labor solely for the benefit of their in-laws. Old men who survived their wives were dependent on their daughters, who inherited the family home. If a man had no daughter, he survived on the charity of other families in the community. As a consequence, the Hopi people valued female children more than male children.

But a Hopi woman's high status did not relieve her of heavy toil. In addition to raising her children, she cooked, made baskets and pottery, tended her garden, and gathered wild plants. She was also responsible for keeping the household supplied with water—a backbreaking chore that might take her down the steep trails from the mesa to springs in the canyon below several times a day. In the summer, when the springs dwin-

Delicate ornaments pierce the ears, nose, and lower lip of a Yupik woman from southern Alaska. The drawing was done by John Webber, a member of Captain James Cook's late-18th-century expeditions.

dled to a trickle, the job of hauling water might take most of the day. The women took turns at the streams, sewing and chatting under the shade of blankets while the water dribbled into their two- to five-gallon clay jugs. As soon as they had trudged up the trail and emptied the jugs into storage vessels, they had to go back down and get in line again.

Corn was the staple food. Each day, Pueblo women spent hours kneeling in front of their grinding stones, pulverizing the kernels into meal. Grinding corn was essential both to life and to a woman's identity. To demonstrate that she was qualified to be a wife, a Hopi girl was required to spend four days grinding corn in the house of her husband-to-be before she was granted permission to marry.

Among the neighboring Navajo, the women also owned most of the property, including the hogans in which they lived and the sheep and goats that were a source of food and of wool for blankets, rugs, and clothing. In large part because of the economic independence they derived from possession of these valuable properties, Navajo women had few restrictions on their activities, and the division of labor was flexible and informal. In individual families, husbands sometimes helped care for the livestock, and the women often helped their men in the fields.

The Apache delineated sexual roles more sharply. Women were expected to tend house, care for children, and procure food, while men hunted, fought, and went on raids to acquire livestock, guns, and other booty.

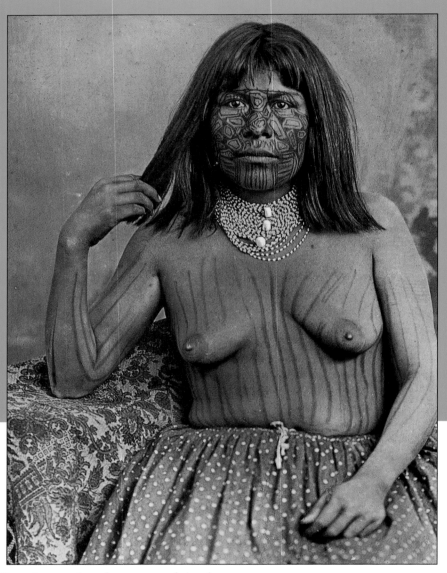

Elaborate facial tattooing and body paint adorn this Mohave woman photographed in 1882. Among the Mohave, facial tattoos indicated a woman's family and status. Many other Native Americans also practiced tattooing, although the custom had begun to decline by the end of the 19th century.

Still, the Apache regarded women as the mainstays of their people, a belief embodied in their lavish female puberty ceremonies.

The high status that was accorded women imposed heavy obligations on married Apache men, who, like Hopi husbands, subordinated themselves to their wives' families. As one Apache man explained: "At marriage a man goes to the camp of the girl's parents to live. We do this because a woman is more valuable than a man. The in-laws depend a great deal on him, for hunting and all kinds of work. He is almost a slave to them. Everything he gets on the hunt goes to them." Typically, Apache hunters found game only sporadically. Women were the main providers, and they maintained an exhaustive store of knowledge about all of the sources of food in their rugged land. Dilth-cleyhen, the daughter of Victorio, a legendary 19th-century Chiricahua Apache warrior, recalled her mother telling her: "Be grateful for our land. It gives us all we have."

In autumn, the women of Dilth-cleyhen's tribe, whose territory covered present-day southwestern New Mexico and southeastern Arizona, dug roots and gathered prickly pears, acorns, piñon nuts, the beans of thorny mesquite, and the banana-like fruit of yucca plants. In the spring

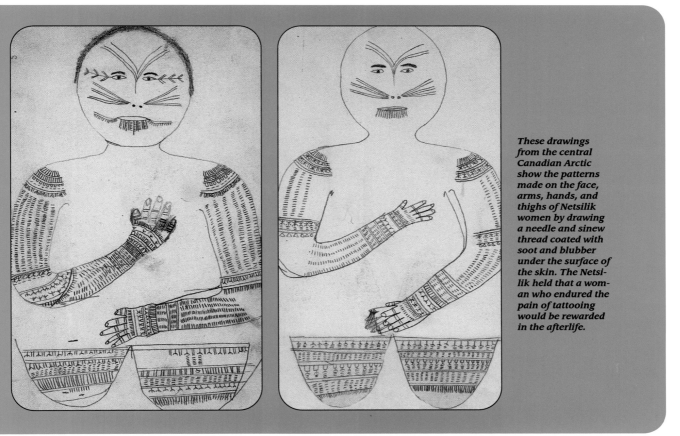

These drawings from the central Canadian Arctic show the patterns made on the face, arms, hands, and thighs of Netsilik women by drawing a needle and sinew thread coated with soot and blubber under the surface of the skin. The Netsilik held that a woman who endured the pain of tattooing would be rewarded in the afterlife.

and summer, they filled their burden baskets with wild onions, greens, grass seeds, berries, and cactus fruits. Women had to keep on the move to gather this sparse and scattered bounty. They knew every source of precious water, and planned family migrations based on their knowledge of ripening wild plants and the movements of small game such as prairie dogs and rabbits. Their word in such matters was law, superseding even the hunting and raiding plans of men.

Chiricahua women were also responsible for the spiritual support of their warriors. Wives sent their men off on raids with cheers and prayers for a safe return; in some Apache groups, the women said a prayer for the warriors every time they pulled a pot off the fire. During the men's absences, wives and children behaved cautiously so as not to bring bad luck on the war party. Dilth-cleyhen, for example, was taught to stack wood neatly, lest pieces of kindling scatter—a bad omen for the men.

Every Chiricahua girl was drilled in the importance of keeping a weapon and a small supply of emergency rations handy at all times. In the event that the band was caught by surprise, she would thus have the necessities for survival. Older girls were taught how to use camouflage, handle horses, and follow tracks. They learned the same fighting skills as the boys—how to use a knife, a bow and arrow, and a rifle—so they could defend themselves and their families during enemy raids.

In the late 1800s, when the Apache were resisting the U.S. Army's attempts to force them onto reservations and yet continuing their ongoing feuds with the Mexicans, many women proved themselves capable fighters. Lozen, the younger sister of Victorio, was a skilled archer and horsewoman, as well as a healer and clairvoyant. She never married but devoted her life to her brother, sitting in on the council fires when war leaders were planning military strategy. Lozen's ability to detect the location of the enemy by a tingling sensation in her palms was believed to have been a factor in Victorio's triumphs. "I see as one from a height sees in every direction," she once said.

In October 1880, Victorio and his band were ambushed by Mexican troops in Tres Castillos, northern Mexico. Lozen was not present, and many Chiricahuas believe that Victorio and his men would have escaped death had she been with them. Lozen went on to fight with Geronimo. The great Apache war leader entrusted her and another woman named Dahteste with the preliminary negotiations of his final surrender to the Americans in 1886. Four years later, Lozen died in a prison camp in Alabama. "Lozen is as my right hand," Victorio once said. "Strong as a man, braver than most, and cunning in strategy, Lozen is a shield to her people."

Out to the west, beyond the Rocky Mountains and toward the Pacific Ocean, Native Americans were largely freed of the persistent threat of want that prevailed in the American Southwest. In California, a temperate climate, many rivers, and fertile soil produced a varied diet that sustained the highest concentration of Indians north of Mexico. Farther up the coast, a lush environment supported lives of near opulence. There, rivers and bays teemed with fish and marine animals. Abundant rainfall nourished great stands of cedar and other trees that provided the raw materials for housing, fuel, and boats. The abundance of these resources allowed tribes as far-flung as the Tlingit of Alaska's southern coast, the Kwakiutl of Vancouver Island, and the Chinook of the Columbia River valley to amass considerable material wealth and develop a complex social hierarchy.

Among these prosperous tribes, the headmen of clans or lineages—and their immediate families—constituted a kind of nobility. Below these "nobles," households were ranked on a descending social scale based on wealth. A family's position was reckoned in terms of the material property it owned or controlled—including housing sites; the rights to local game, fish, berries, and timber; as well as heirloom objects and the personal

Buffalo headdresses adorn two middle-aged Cheyenne women, who once performed as Buffalo Dancers in a healing ceremony called the Massaum. In many tribes, women became more involved in ceremonial life— and thus gained more prestige—as they matured.

names associated with the family crests displayed on the towering totem poles outside each home.

A woman's life was influenced by her position in this system. Wealthy, high-ranking women often had slaves to help them with their work, which revolved around gathering wild plants and processing and storing fish, particularly salmon. The ready availability of these resources ensured all women a certain amount of leisure to devote to gracious living.

Coastal women spent a great deal of their time cooking and were known for their cuisine. Boiling, broiling, roasting, and steaming were all in their culinary repertoire. Food was handsomely served, dished up from hardwood or basketry platters and bowls, with spoons and dippers fashioned from sheep and goat horn. More elaborate utensils were brought out for feasts—spoons carved with family crests and inlaid with abalone, beautifully carved bentwood boxes, and bowls with decorated lids.

Pacific Coast tribes were normally headed by males. Married women belonged to their husbands' families, and men, for the most part, were the owners of the family property. The women, however, had considerable control over these resources. Tlingit women in particular were shrewd managers of wealth. When a woman married, she assumed control of her husband's treasury. She was responsible for maintaining the family wealth, including the objects laid away for potlatches—the lavish feasts in which families burnished the honor of their lineages by giving away piles of gifts. In the winter, women added to the family treasuries by crafting basketry hats or weaving blankets—items that could be either traded or added to the stock of potlatch gifts.

Tlingit women were noted for being hard bargainers, and their opinions were rarely disregarded by the men. "I bought a silver-fox skin from Tsa-tate, but his wife made him return the articles of trade and recover the skin," wrote one disgruntled European fur trader in 1882. "In the same way, I was perpetually being annoyed by having to undo bargains because his wife said 'clekh,' that is, no."

Women generally held less sway among the California Indians. In most of the dozens of major tribal groups there, men were regarded as the heads of their families. Wives took up residence with their husbands' people, and descent was almost universally traced through the male line. Moreover, men controlled most of the valuable property. The rights to sections of land and their resources were held communally as the property of male lineages, giving men the upper hand economically. In general, a woman was in control of her own food gathering, child rearing, and house

The women's auxiliary of the Kiowa Tonkonga, or Black Legs, warrior society meets for a ceremony. Traditionally, most female societies centered on crafts, although the Kiowa had one known as Old Women, whose much esteemed members were consulted by warriors both before and after raids.

management duties, and had the right to keep for herself or dispose of whatever she produced in the way of clothing, ornaments, and household utensils. Otherwise she had little power other than the influence she might wield over her husband in the privacy of their own home.

Publicly, the women of most California communities were expected to defer to their husbands and to work hard. Tolowa men on the verge of marriage were advised to examine their intended brides' hands carefully; the more rough and scratched a woman's palms were, the more industrious a wife she would make. On trails, wives followed a respectful few paces behind their husbands. In some groups, the sexes even dined apart.

California women generally played little role in political life. One exception was among the Pomo—where the usual line of succession was through the headman's eldest sister. Women assumed political leadership in their own right in other California tribes, but only under certain circumstances. A Miwok daughter could succeed to her father's chiefdom, for ex-

ample, if there were no sons. Or the widow of a Miwok chief might serve as regent for her son until he reached maturity. The sister of a deceased Yuki chief sometimes assumed office temporarily until a suitable male successor could be found. Throughout most of the region, women were also barred from participating in major religious festivals.

California Indian women had one route to status and material wealth available to them—as medical practitioners. Women healers were found throughout the region. In northern California, among the Yurok, Karok, Maidu, Miwok, Achumawi, Wiyot, and Shasta, women dominated the healing profession. As with Native Americans living elsewhere on the continent, their practice of medicine blended the natural and the supernatural. Many ailments, from earaches, blisters, and snakebite to the pangs of childbirth, were responsive to natural remedies. As agriculturists, almost all California Indian women had a working knowledge of herbal remedies. Particularly talented herbalists were able to draw on much of the plant kingdom as a natural pharmacy and to produce medicines to alleviate the symptoms of most common ills.

But all illnesses were also regarded as having a lesser or greater spiritual component—usually perceived as the presence in the body of some hostile foreign element. The curing of disease involved identifying and removing the malevolent entity. This was the province of shamans. In most California groups, these spiritual healers diagnosed disease by singing, dancing, or smoking—sometimes to the point of entering trancelike states until they could locate the offending object. They then ritually removed it by placing their mouths on the patient's body and sucking out the disease.

Male or female, healers acquired their vocation as the result of being possessed by a spirit or having experienced a vision. In many California tribes, such as the Wailaki, Maidu, and Yokuts, the calling was likely to come in the form of a conversation with a supernatural being during a trance. Among the Cahuilla, future shamans were identified by means of repeated dreams, usually starting in childhood. Shamans among the Wiyot acquired their powers through visions that they received during nighttime vigils on mountaintops.

Shamanistic dreams generally came unsolicited, although a woman who wished to become a healer could try to evoke the requisite visions by solitary fasting. The dreams, however, would appear only if such a path had been foreordained. As Ruby Modesto, a Cahuilla medicine woman, or *pul,* stated: "A real pul is born, destined to be one. It's a calling. You are chosen by Umna'ah, our Creator. He makes you a pul in the womb."

Four generations of Navajo women pose against the background of their southwestern homeland. Like their ancestors, these modern women live and work together, with the older members of the family passing down their knowledge and wisdom to the younger.

An aged Navajo woman cradles her great-grandchild. Native American youngsters have always learned about their culture and heritage through stories told them by their female elders.

A Crow child recently embarked on life's pathway nestles in the arms of a kinswoman, Amelia Passes, whose own journey is nearing its conclusion.

Once a woman received the calling, she usually served an apprenticeship under an experienced shaman. A Yurok healer gained her skills through years of strenuous initiation rites during which a spirit would enter her body and leave behind an animate object that was the physical manifestation of its power. This was referred to as a "pain." The pain would induce trances and illnesses in the apprentice until she gained control of it through prolonged dancing and fasting. Once she had conquered the pain—learning to regurgitate and swallow it at will—she could use it to heal, drawing it up to employ its power. The learning process could cover a span of several years, as the apprentice acquired control over a succession of pains. In practice, she would place her mouth on an ailing person's body until one of her pains penetrated the patient and wrapped itself around the cause of the illness. She would then suck it out.

The rewards for undergoing such rigors were considerable. Yurok doctors were women of prestige, and they were highly paid in dentalium shells for their services. Because of the special power associated with menstruation, most medicine women were past middle age—even if they had received their calling and been trained for it as girls. Many tribes believed that herbal remedies lost their efficacy if dispensed by a menstruating woman—and that a fertile woman's life-giving powers might clash with certain powers that brought about healing. Menopause freed women from such restrictions.

For a great many Native American women, the end of their childbearing years marked an important passage into a different realm of respect and power. Old age in general was synonymous with wisdom. Older women frequently assumed new ritual duties, and their views on important tribal issues carried added weight. Above all, however, female elders were valued as the keepers of tribal history. Busy young mothers, their days filled with gathering and preparing food, often turned over a great deal of the day-to-day care of their offspring to grandmothers. Tending to their descendants' well-being while instilling in them the values and ancient traditions of their people, Indian women completed their lives by starting off new generations in the path of their ancestors. ✦

MOTHER OF US ALL

During the Green Corn Ceremony, seven Cherokee women carry baskets of the first ripened vegetables of the season, including corn. In this painting set in precontact times by a Cherokee artist, the women represent Selu, the female spirit who first provided corn.

"She is mother of us all, in fertility, in holding, in taking us again back to her breast"—these words begin a Keres ceremonial prayer. Whether she is known by the people of Laguna Pueblo as Mother Earth, by the Iroquois as Sky Woman, or by the Inuit as Sedna, a female spirit pervades the lore of almost every Indian tribe from the eastern seaboard to the Pacific Coast. While most of the tribes also honor Father Sky or some other paternal creator, legendary women seem to play even more prominent roles than their male counterparts in the daily lives of many Native American peoples.

The Navajo and the neighboring Apache peoples trace their ancestry back to the mysterious Changing Woman, who continues to act as a guardian of fertility and reproduction as well as a dispenser of great medicine power. Female supernaturals in a variety of forms have also acted as sacred envoys and gift givers. The Lakota Sioux look to a beautiful messenger by the name of White Buffalo Calf Woman as the source of their

centuries-old Sacred Pipe, an object of importance in their ceremonial life. The Shawnee honor a creator known as Our Grandmother, who not only begot the first people but also taught them to dance and gave them their code of behavior.

Most Indian communities credit legendary women with being the original providers of one of the world's most hallowed treasures, corn. Unrivaled as a food source, corn also has great spiritual significance, serving as a holy offering and a medium for anointing priests. The Zuni and some of their neighbors owe thanks to the Six Corn Maidens for this vital crop, while the Iroquois honor the Three Sisters for bestowing the grain—as well as squash and beans.

One of the best-known corn givers is Selu, whose name comes from the Cherokee word for maize. The first woman, she bore two sons and nourished them with ample supplies of corn and beans from her magical storehouse. One day the curious boys decided to spy on her as she retrieved the food. Through a hole in the wall, they watched her rub her stomach and produce ears of corn from between her legs. Then she bared her breast and coaxed green beans from her nipples. Aghast at such sorcery, the boys decided to kill her. Before she died, Selu instructed the youngsters to clear the land in front of her cabin and drag her corpse around the clearing seven times in order to ensure an abundant and endless supply of grain for her descendants. The lazy boys did a poor job of clearing, however, and dragged her body around the area only twice. As a consequence, corn grows only in scattered areas of the Cherokee's native Appalachia, and it requires cultivation.

Although murdered by her sons, Selu lives on at the end of the world and has even welcomed the delinquent boys into her new home. Like other sacred women, she will remain there always, watching over her people, for, as the Ojibwa claim: "Woman is forever, eternal. Man comes from woman and to woman he returns."

WHITE BUFFALO CALF WOMAN

A painting by a 19th-century Cheyenne artist depicts White Buffalo Calf Woman delivering the Sacred Pipe to a hunter, as an eagle with a rattlesnake in its mouth bears witness to the transfer. White Buffalo Calf Woman's message spread rapidly from the Lakota to neighboring Plains tribes.

Ages ago, according to one version of a Lakota story, a beautiful maiden appeared to their ancestors on the Great Plains, carrying a pipe and a stone. She explained to them that her pipe bowl represented the earth, that the wood stem symbolized all growing things, that the buffalo carved on the bowl stood for all land animals, and that the pipe's 12 eagle feathers signified all winged creatures. Whoever prayed with this pipe would be in harmony with the universe, she instructed. And the seven circles incised on her round stone represented the seven holy rites that were to be observed by the Lakota people forever. After disclosing the mysteries, the maiden was transformed into a white buffalo calf and disappeared into a large herd, leaving only her medicine bundle and sacred teachings behind.

Marie Louise Defender (right), a Sioux woman, smokes a pipe modeled after the one
described in legend as that of White Buffalo
Calf Woman. Defender (below), holding a
buffalo skull, represents White Buffalo Calf
Woman during the Sun Dance Ceremony.

Alex White Plume stands on the plains of South
Dakota with part of the sacred buffalo herd believed to be descended from the one that White
Buffalo Calf Woman joined following her
metamorphosis. The Oglala people hope the
herd will someday produce a white buffalo calf.

A photograph taken in 1892 shows the interior of a Lakota initiation lodge that has been prepared for a girl's puberty rite, one of the seven rituals passed down by White Buffalo Calf Woman. Performed after the girl's first menstrual period, the ceremony teaches the meaning of change and the responsibilities of womanhood.

Leonard Crow Dog, a Sioux, prepares to practice another of the original rituals, the Inipi, or Sweat Lodge Ceremony, by entering a steam-filled sapling tent. One participant has likened the experience to a return to "the warm womb of Mother Earth" in which he shares "the lifeblood of the world" as his sweat mingles with that of his companions.

Modern Sioux honor a dead relative with a Memorial Giveaway Ceremony at Fort Peck, Montana. Usually held on the anniversary of the death, the ceremony is an age-old tradition among Sioux people and is considered by the Lakota to be one of the rites given by White Buffalo Calf Woman.

THE SHAWNEE'S GRANDMOTHER

The Shawnee of Oklahoma honor a holy woman named Our Grandmother, who received assistance from the Great Spirit in creating humankind after being the only survivor of a terrible flood. She gave the Shawnee life, as well as a code of ethics and most of their religious ceremonies. Today she lives in a celestial bark house where she weaves a huge basket. At night a mischievous puppy, aided by her grandson, unravels the work. But someday she will finish, and when she does, the world will end. Then the basket will tumble to earth and enclose for eternity all the faithful who have kept her laws and ceremonies.

The Shawnee believe she likes to see her grandchildren dance, so they continue to perform the songs and steps she taught them. And on special occasions, an extra voice, that of the Grandmother, is said to join in the singing.

These two paintings by Shawnee artists depict versions of the Pumpkin Dance, one segment of the Bread Dance, a joyful prayer to Our Grandmother for crops and fertility. At left, Shawnees conveyed by mule and wagon gather at a dance ground about 1910 in Oklahoma. Above, contemporary Shawnees move in a circle, led by a dancer carrying a turkey tail-feather fan (inset).

This stylized painting includes five women carrying baskets of corn on their heads. The women are participating in a Shalako Ceremony, which is part of the most important event of the Zuni sacred calendar.

CORN MAIDENS OF THE ZUNI

According to tribal lore, the first Zunis to settle in the Southwest survived on a modest diet of grass until the Sun sent them the Six Corn Maidens. The beautiful sisters danced among the grasses, transforming them into maize. The first plant they touched burned with a yellow flame; the second sent clouds of blue smoke into the air; the third ignited and became a glowing red ember. The fire reached its zenith at the fourth plant, sending forth a white-hot flame; at the fifth it produced multicolored sparks; and it sputtered out at the sixth,

leaving only black ashes. Thus the six colors of corn known to the Zuni—yellow, blue, red, white, speckled, and black—came into the world.

Eventually, however, the Zuni began to waste the corn. Hurt by such careless treatment, the Corn Maidens left the village. After several years, the forgiving sisters returned to bless the crop, but they no longer danced among the stalks as in olden times. Today many Pueblo communities select young women to represent the Corn Maidens at their festivals to render the harvest holy.

A woman holds two ears of sacred corn, one blue and one white, during a religious celebration at Santa Clara Pueblo. Corn plays an essential role in many Pueblo sacred rites.

The kachina Ahulani is flanked by his two sisters, Yellow Corn Girl and Blue Corn Girl for Soyal, the Hopi New Year. Representatives of the Hopi corn spirits appear during the winter solstice to celebrate the return of the sun from its southward migration.

Holding an ear of corn and pine boughs in each hand, a Tewa girl at San Juan Pueblo impersonates a Corn Maiden while performing a ceremonial dance. She wears a colorful eagle-feather headdress that symbolizes the rainbows and clouds necessary for rain and a bountiful harvest.

CHANGING WOMAN

The Navajo have related the story of Changing Woman for generations. Born of the mingling of darkness and dawn, Changing Woman was adopted by First Man and First Woman, who raised her according to the directions of the Holy People. When she reached maturity four days after birth, her parents arranged a Kinaalda, or puberty ceremony, which is still practiced. Imbued with the generative power of the female, Changing Woman created the corn plant and later mixed scrapings of her own skin with cornmeal to create the First People, ancestors of the Navajo. She continues to favor the tribe with her presence at ceremonies, including the sacred Blessingway, which she gave to her people.

A painting (below) by Navajo artist Gerald Nailor entitled "The Sun God and His Wife" depicts the Sun impregnating Changing Woman. Before creating the Navajo, she gave birth to twin sons, Monster Slayer and Child Born of Water, who cleared the world of fiends.

A sand painting (left) from the Blessingway ceremony is intended to ensure good crops. Changing Woman stands between stalks of corn and above a cross symbolizing Mother Earth.

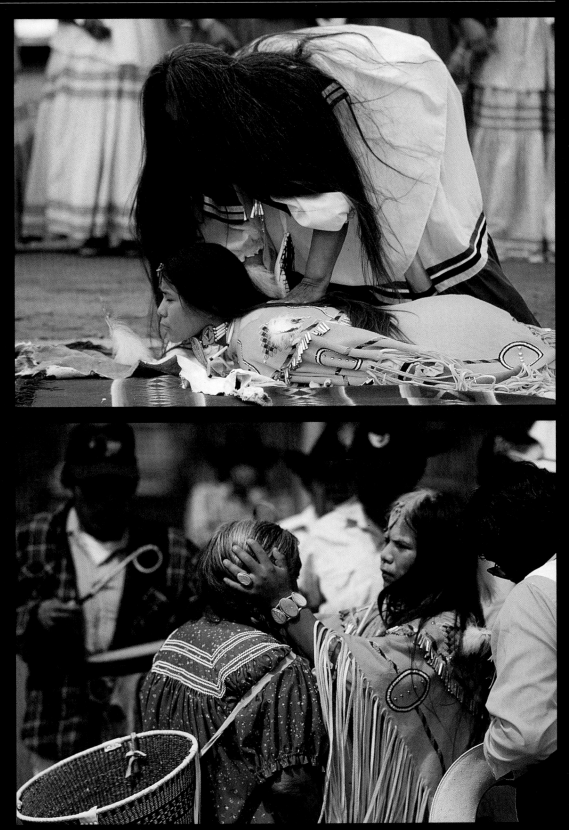

A sponsor molds an adolescent girl into the likeness of Changing Woman at a Navajo puberty ritual, the Kinaalda. The direct translation of Changing Woman's Navajo name is Woman She Becomes Time and Again, indicating the perpetual cycle that is celebrated at every Kinaalda.

Suffused with healing power in the course of her four-day coming-of-age ceremony, the girl extends her arms to cure a sick woman. Her face has been painted with corn pollen as part of a ceremonial blessing.

THE FEMALE DOMAIN

When they saw that Native American women did much of the strenuous physical labor within their communities, European observers often wrongly assumed that Indian cultures considered women inferior beings who existed solely for the convenience of men. "All the hard work falls upon the women," wrote one 19th-century missionary to the Ojibwa people, "so that it may be truly said of them, that they are the slaves of their husbands."

What many Europeans failed to understand, however, was that by performing tasks crucial to the well-being of the family, Indian women existed as equals, not inferiors. Indeed, women's work—from making clothing to collecting daily stores of firewood and water to producing the major portion of the family's food supplies—was highly valued in Native American societies. Doing it well brought women honor and prestige.

Native American women often had complete dominion over the family house—even the choice of its site. Among many Indian societies, including the Pueblo groups shown at right, women not only ran the house, they also owned the dwelling itself and the family's property. The more skilled a woman became at producing goods, whether food, clothing, pottery, blankets, or jewelry, the more social and economic power she wielded—a condition that a few non-Indian observers were shrewd enough to recognize. Family life for North America's Indians, noted Joseph Nicollet, a perceptive scientist-explorer who spent time among the Ojibwa during the early 1800s, was "not a matter of one sex having power over the other," but one of mutual dependence and respect.

Balancing a full water jug on her head, a Zuni woman returns home in this photograph taken about 1890. Zuni and other Pueblo women retrieved water for their households several times each day.

A young woman fires freshly made clay pots and bowls under heated slabs of animal manure. She uses a long pole to keep the pottery covered. Other pots, which will be fired later, have been positioned near the heat to dry.

A woman bakes bread in an "horno," a beehive-shaped adobe oven. Women built the ovens themselves, covering the adobe with a homemade whitewash that was made from ground gypsum and dung chips.

Two women plaster the walls of an adobe house with mud to seal small cracks and chinks. Pueblo men and women worked together to build their houses. Men erected the walls and roof beams; women plastered the walls and covered the roof with grass, brushwood, and mud.

THE SEMINOLE

Among various Native American peoples, including the Seminole of what is now southern Florida, the female lineage predominated. After marriage, a Seminole couple usually went to live near the house, or chickee *(right),* of the wife's mother. Any children born to the couple belonged to their mother's clan. Although fathers had close relationships with their children, it was their wives' brothers—the children's maternal uncles—who were responsible for their training. Young boys learned how to fish, hunt, and prepare for war from these uncles, not from their fathers.

Because all property was inherited through the clan lines, a Seminole woman owned her family's house and almost all its belongings. Should a woman want a divorce, she just placed a bundle of her husband's personal items outside their dwelling. He then moved back into his mother's house or into the house of his second wife, if he had one. A Seminole man could take a second wife—but only with the permission of his first wife, who was always acknowledged as the principal wife.

A Seminole woman grates the roots of the wontie plant, a wild palmlike vegetable found in the American Southeast. The grated roots were often added as a thickener to a corn soup known as "sofke."

Built about 1900, this traditional open-sided Seminole house, called a chickee, has an interior platform raised about 30 inches off the ground to protect its inhabitants and their belongings from the muddy aftermath of Florida's rainstorms.

With the aid of a hand-operated sewing machine, a Seminole woman joins together colorful bands of cloth that will be made into a skirt or shirt. The advent of sewing machines in the late 1800s helped women fashion the multicolored patchwork clothing that became distinctive of the Seminole.

Two Seminole women pound corn kernels into meal in a hollowed log. Women spent hours making cornmeal, which they used in a variety of breads, soups, drinks, and other dishes.

THE NAVAJO

Whenever the members of a Navajo family built themselves a new "home place," or hogan *(above),* they sang blessings to ensure that all who lived within its walls would do so peacefully and safely. Even though the exact wording of the songs may have varied from family to family, they always acknowledged the woman's predominant position within the home.

The hogan was her domain, the place where she cooked, cleaned, prayed, cared for the children, and made all the clothing, rugs, baskets, and other household items. Although the work was often physically exhausting, it earned the woman significant status. She controlled the material possessions of the family, including its valuable flock of sheep, which she tended with the help of her family.

The Navajo people constructed their hogans in small camps. Each camp contained several related families that were presided over by a "head mother," or matriarch. Much as her female descendants were responsible for their own hogans, this head mother was in charge of the camp as a whole and had the final say in all family matters.

Friends and family gather around a weaver at her loom, while other women card and spin outside a hogan, the traditional dome-shaped Navajo dwelling made of earth and timber. Women frequently sang as they wove their hand-dyed sheeps wool into intricately patterned rugs and blankets.

Adorned with silver jewelry, two Navajo shepherdesses keep hold of some lambs and a little child under their care. Women, accompanied by their children, often walked miles each day to find adequate grassland and water for their flocks.

A woman spreads out peaches to dry under the hot southwestern sun. Preserving foods for the family's use was an essential task for Navajo women.

A woman buries a newly woven blanket under damp sand to flatten it. After several days, the curled edges created during looming will be gone, and the blanket will be ready to use.

THE OJIBWA

Among the Ojibwa people of the upper Midwest, women had dominion not only over their wigwams, or homes, but also over their family's wild rice beds, maple sugar groves, corn plantings, and even the deer and other game their husbands brought back from their hunts. The hunter's "feeling of honor insists that he must first of all consult with his wife how the deer is to be divided among his neighbors and friends," noted Johann Kohl, a German writer who visited the Ojibwa in the mid-1800s.

Few activities were off-limits to Ojibwa women. They frequently accompanied their husbands to the hunting grounds, sometimes skinning and processing the meat on the spot. They also fished alongside the men. But most of the women's time was spent gathering rice, berries, and other wild plants; tapping maple trees for sap; and planting, weeding, and harvesting corn.

Ojibwa women could even aspire to become part of a select group of skilled healers known as the Midewiwin, or Grand Medicine Society. Membership in the society required an arduous apprenticeship but ultimately brought power and prestige to the initiates.

Above, a woman weaves stalks into a mat to be used as a floor covering. Similar mats were used to cover the frame of a wigwam (right). It was a woman's job to transport the mats to each new campsite and to attach them to the wigwam's frame.

A couple pose for a photograph outside their wigwam, covered with large sheets of bark. In Ojibwa society, the wife kept the dwelling and controlled all activities within and around it. She even told family members where to sleep and store their personal items.

An Ojibwa woman tends kettles of boiling maple sap in this photograph taken about 1900. In early spring, family groups moved from their winter villages to temporary sugar camps, where the women were largely responsible for producing maple sugar, an important part of the Ojibwa diet.

THE PLAINS TRIBES

The building of a tipi, the portable home of the Plains Indians, was strictly woman's work. Under the guidance of an experienced female "lodge maker," Plains women worked together to stitch enough buffalo hides—sometimes as many as two dozen of them—for the tipi's outer covering. The stitching was a festive occasion, hosted by the woman who owned the hides and would eventually own the finished tipi.

Whenever a family moved, the wife was responsible for dismantling and transporting the tipi and for pitching it at the new location. A beautiful, well-made tipi brought honor and prestige to the wife. Plains women told of the fine tipis they had created and cared for, much as their husbands recounted their brave deeds as hunters or warriors.

Using a flesher, a special tool typically made from elk horn and metal, a Sioux woman scrapes a buffalo hide. Women skilled at preparing a hide—a task that could take up to 10 days—were greatly admired.

A Sioux woman plucks quills from a porcupine carcass. Women softened and dyed the quills before they used them to adorn clothing, moccasins, or other items.

Accompanied by young children, including two tucked snugly inside a covered travois, a Cheyenne woman prepares for the trip to her family's next campsite. The long poles doubled as tipi supports.

Blackfeet women erect a tipi on a grassy encampment. Women working together could set up a tipi and install the family's belongings within an hour.

2

A BRIDGE BETWEEN TWO WORLDS

Two Apache mothers display their sleeping infants in a studio photograph taken in the 1880s. The children are strapped into traditional cradleboards of wood and hide.

By the early 18th century, Indian peoples living in the eastern third of North America had become caught up in a web of trade. In Florida, the Spaniards had established a mission system that spread Catholicism and extracted foodstuffs and animal skins from more than 100 Indian villages. In Canada, French missionaries and fur traders had extended the reach of New France to the regions around and beyond the Great Lakes, while their compatriots in America explored the lower Mississippi River and founded the colony of Louisiana. The British, meanwhile, had supplanted the Dutch in the Hudson and Delaware River valleys and set up thriving colonies in Virginia, New England, and the Carolinas.

The attractive products of European industry that the Indians had once considered luxuries were rapidly becoming commonplace. The men hunted and fought with guns rather than bows and arrows; the women tilled their gardens with hoes of iron instead of stone, cooked in kettles of brass instead of clay, and sewed clothes of cloth instead of animal skins, using needles made of steel instead of bone. As the Indians grew increasingly dependent on European manufactures, some native technologies were forgotten and lost forever. Tribes that were well equipped with firearms and metal tools possessed a military and economic advantage that had to be matched by other tribes. The competition for trade goods had become a battle for survival.

A number of the smaller tribes crumbled under the strain. Some of them vanished completely; others moved farther west or merged with more powerful neighbors. Many of the indigenous peoples, however, were able to adapt to this changing world and maintain varying degrees of independence for most of the century. And their ability to endure was attributable in no small part to their women, who served their people not only as preservers of tribal institutions but also as bridge builders to the foreign cultures. European chroniclers tended to focus their attention on the actions and achievements of the male war chiefs and peacemakers, but in many instances, it was the anonymous Native American women who held their communities together.

As a consequence of the relative stability of traditional female roles, Indian women experienced less disruption in their daily lives than did Indian men. As the fur trade consumed their way of life, the young men frequently had to spend months away from home, searching the forests for game—not for sustenance, as was the case in the past, but to collect pelts to feed the voracious trading system. At times they had to go to war, fighting other tribes over disputed hunting grounds or in support of a European ally trying to gain an advantage in the trade. The women, in the meantime, remained behind and carried on much as they had always done: caring for the children, growing crops, gathering wild foods, tanning hides, and reinforcing old bonds with family elders.

At the same time, a large number of women created new links for the community by marrying traders who came into their territory. The marriages drew the newcomers into Indian kinship circles and affirmed the tribe's economic and political ties with the white colonies. Cree families, for example, often reserved at least one of their daughters to offer as a wife to the traders who did business with them. And Creek and Cherokee headmen commonly sealed their alliances with a particular European power by arranging a marriage between a niece or other close clanswoman and a trader or colonial official.

By acting as interpreters and advisers to two sets of men—their white husbands and their clan relatives—many of these women expanded their influence and rose in status. Some of them—the Creek Mary Musgrove, the Mohawk Molly Brant, and the Cherokee Nancy Ward, for example—became legendary figures in both white and Indian worlds. Through their efforts to reconcile the cultures of whites and Indians, these remarkable women made their indelible marks before being swept away, along with their kinspeople far and wide, in the inexorable tide of white encroachment. Down through history, their lives serve to amplify the long struggle of Native American people to retain their freedom and independence.

The Creek woman Cousaponokeesa was born into the prestigious Wind Clan in the year 1700 at the Lower Creek settlement of Coweta, located in the piny woods along the banks of the Ocmulgee River near the modern city of Macon, Georgia. Like other southeastern peoples, Creek clans trace their lineage back through their mothers to a common ancestor, usually a totem bird, fish, or animal. Cousaponokeesa's clan birth was especially

A white trapper takes the hand of his Indian bride in this highly romanticized picture painted in 1845 by Alfred Jacob Miller. Many tribes encouraged such marriages to strengthen social and trade relations with outsiders.

auspicious. As a member of the Wind Clan, she was descended from a group of spirit beings known as the Wind People. For as long as anyone could remember, the human progeny of the Wind People had held certain types of leadership positions in the 50-odd Upper and Lower Towns that made up the Creek Confederacy. Cousaponokeesa's mother was an esteemed clan matriarch, the sister of Hoboyelty, the influential *miko,* or civil chief, of Coweta, whom the Europeans called Emperor Brims. Another of her mother's brothers was Chekilli, Coweta's "great warrior," or war chief. The identity of Cousaponokeesa's father is unknown. Legend has it that he was a Scottish or English trader.

Presented to a revered Osage woman by her people, this flannel robe retains its rich red coloring, which is sacred and symbolizes life. Many Plains tribes honor their outstanding women by awarding them finely crafted garments to wear.

In Cousaponokeesa's day, little Creek girls were taught traditional female skills by older female clan members. Included among these skills were gardening, pounding corn, preserving foodstuffs, making cane baskets, processing animal hides, and gathering the holly shrub that was used to make black drink, the ritual tea Creeks traditionally consumed before setting out on important undertakings. Cousaponokeesa's principal instructor was her mother's eldest sister. English speakers would call such a relative an aunt. But to a Creek child, she was likened to the parent and addressed by the term "little mother."

At the time of her birth, Cousaponokeesa's people were surrounded by enemies. With the founding of the colony of Carolina by a group of British merchants in 1670 on land that the Spaniards claimed, the Creek became enmeshed in the European rivalry for New World hegemony. In addition, they were menaced by hostile Indian neighbors—the Cherokee to the north, the Chickasaw to the northwest, and the Apalachee to the south—who, like the Creek, were vying with one another for advantageous trade alliances with the Europeans. Perhaps a decade before the birth of Cousaponokeesa, the Coweta Creeks moved their town east from a site along the Chattahoochee River to the Ocmulgee River in order to be closer to the Carolina traders, their principal source of guns, ammunition, and other essential goods. When Cousaponokeesa was a young girl, possibly as part of an effort to maintain amicable relations with the Carolinians, her clan sent her to live with a white family in Pomponne, a small settlement located on the outskirts of Charles Towne (modern-day Charleston, South Carolina). It was there that she attended an English school, was baptized in a church, and was given the Christian name of Mary.

While Mary was living with the whites, Indian outrage against corrupt and abusive Carolina trading practices erupted into a widespread revolt that united the majority of the southeastern tribes. The British referred to the insurrection either as Brims' War, because Brims was the principal architect of the Indian alliance, or as the Yamasee War, after the first tribe to attack them. When a large war party led by Chekilli crossed the Edisto River at Pomponne and threatened Charles Towne in August 1715, Mary seized the opportunity to run away from her English hosts and join her uncle's forces. After the Carolina militia rallied and drove off the Indians, Mary returned home to Coweta.

Although the Indians initially held the upper hand in the fighting, it soon became obvious that the Carolinians could not be defeated without the marshaling of a total pan-Indian effort. Brims decided to send emissaries to his rivals, the Cherokee, to urge them to join the alliance. The Creek mission ended in disaster, however, when a pro-British Cherokee faction murdered the Coweta ambassadors. This act of perfidy ignited a feud between the Creek and the Cherokee that continued on and off for the next four decades, and it forced Brims to sue for peace. After negotiating a settlement that reestablished commercial links with Carolina, the miko gave his teenage niece in marriage to John Musgrove Jr., the son of an Indian woman and an important Carolina landowner. The union served as a reaffirmation of Creek friendship. For Mary's part, the marriage provided a springboard that enabled her to achieve enormous influence both with her own people and with the white colonists.

During the first seven years of their marriage, Mary and John Musgrove lived among the Creeks, but eventually they moved to the Musgrove estate in Pomponne. In 1732, with the blessings of the South Carolina gov-

An Ojibwa widow cradles a spirit bundle filled with her husband's effects. At the conclusion of her mourning period, she gave the bundle to her dead spouse's relatives.

RITES OF MOURNING AND WIDOWHOOD

In all Native American cultures, it was important for family members to show respect for the dead by following certain rituals. The women of many tribes mourned the death of their spouses for a year or even longer. Rituals of grief varied from group to group. Widows in some Plains tribes cut their hair short, wailed, and slashed their bodies as a means of ensuring that their dead mates would have a safe journey to the afterworld. The Cheyenne, Arapaho, and Blackfeet burned the family tipi and dispersed its contents. A Mandan widow communed with the remains of her husband and offered him the best cooked food as if he were still alive. In the Northwest, widows wore special hats and rubbed ashes on their faces. After the period of mourning had expired, most Indian women resumed the normal rhythms of daily life. They were usually expected to remarry soon, for their skills remained vital to the welfare of the community.

Pledging respect for her dead husband, a Crow widow wears her hair cropped just below her ears.

Skulls of the dead form a circle around the skulls of a male and a female buffalo and two offering poles in a Mandan cemetery. Those who have died more recently lie bundled on wooden scaffolds in the background.

ernor and the Creek leadership, the couple set up a trading post near the mouth of the Savannah River. They called it The Cowpen because of the livestock business they had started to complement their trade in deerskins.

When James Edward Oglethorpe arrived from England the following year to found the crown colony of Georgia, he sought out Mary to serve as his official interpreter and adviser. Her clan connections and fluency in English as well as the Creek languages of Muskogee and Hitchiti made her uniquely qualified to serve as an intermediary between the colonists and the Indians. Now in her thirties, Mary was described at the time as being about five feet tall, with broad cheekbones and luxuriant black hair, which she wore in long braids down her back. Like most Creek women of the period, she dressed in garments fashioned of trade cloth—an osnaburg shift and a red stroud petticoat—rather than animal skins, and wore a decorative ring of trade beads around her forehead.

Existing treaties forbade the colonists from settling south of the Savannah River. But Oglethorpe was undeterred. The land that interested him the most was an area occupied by the Yamacraws, a small band of Creeks and a few Yamasees who had been banished from Coweta, possibly for failing to support Brims during the Yamasee War. The Yamacraws were led by one

An elderly Pomo woman sits in the doorway of her dwelling, which is made of marsh grass, holding an openwork burden basket. The Pomo frequently bartered their basketry for tools, weapons, shells, and furs.

of Mary's clansmen, an old miko named Tomochichi. Recognizing that the interests of the vastly outnumbered Indians would be better served by cooperating with the British rather than resisting them, Mary agreed to help Oglethorpe negotiate a trade and land cession agreement with Tomochichi, and later with other Creek headmen. These new treaties led to the founding of Savannah at the mouth of the Savannah River in 1733 and two years later of Augusta on a bluff upstream at the river's fall line, an ideal site for carrying goods into and out of the Creek homeland.

That same year, John Musgrove died, leaving Mary with a 500-acre

plantation, a large number of cattle and horses, 10 indentured servants, and a thriving deerskin trade. Not only was Mary taking in 12,000 pounds of deerskins annually from the Indians, she was also the main supplier of beef to the colonists. She had become the wealthiest woman on the Georgia frontier, and during the course of the next several years, her influence among both Indians and whites soared.

At the time that Spanish machinations threatened to overturn the Creek-Georgia alliance, Oglethorpe asked Mary to establish a new trading station closer to Florida that could double as a listening post. From there, he hoped that she and her supporters could keep tabs on the Spaniards and their Indian allies. The post, which Mary called Mount Venture, was located about 85 miles southwest of Savannah at the fork where the Ocmulgee and Oconee Rivers join to form the Altamaha River. Soon afterward, Mary married for a second time. Her new husband was Jacob Matthews, an Englishman who was 10 years her junior and a former indentured servant of her first husband. Matthews had been sent to defend Mount Venture with a force of Georgia rangers.

Mary worked hard to hold the Creek-Georgia alliance together. In 1739 she traveled with Oglethorpe to Coweta, where she urged a vast gathering of Indians to spurn Spanish overtures and renew their pact of friendship with the British. Shortly afterward, fighting broke out between Spain and Britain. The Creek sided with the Georgians, thanks in large measure to Mary's influence. The decisive battle took place on July 7, 1742. Oglethorpe, at the head of a joint 600-man Creek-Georgian army, routed a Spanish force attempting to capture the coastal island of Saint Simons at the mouth of the Altamaha River. The following year, when Oglethorpe left Georgia for good, he expressed his appreciation to Mary in dramatic fashion by taking a diamond ring off his own finger and presenting it to her, along with a bank note for £200.

But British gratitude went only so far. During the years that Mary devoted to helping maintain peaceful relations between the Georgians and the Creek, she became the center of a land dispute that threatened to destroy all that she had worked for. The controversy began in 1737, when her kinsman Tomochichi transferred to her landholdings that the Georgians had recognized as belonging to the Yamacraws and thus rightfully his to convey. As a result of these transactions and others involving her cousin Malatchi, the new miko of Coweta, Mary claimed ownership of thousands of square miles of land along the Savannah River as well as the offshore islands of Sapelo, Ossabaw, and Saint Catherines.

Her assertion presented the British with a legal quandary that would trouble Georgia for more than two decades. Traditionally, the southeastern Indians had no concept of private land ownership. But years of experience in dealing with whites had instructed them in the matter of European notions of property. While Oglethorpe and his associates had no problem accepting the right of Creek headmen to transfer lands to the British Crown, these same Englishmen were loath to recognize the prerogative of these same headmen to transfer lands to an individual Indian. At the same time, they were afraid to antagonize Mary, because her goodwill was essential to the survival of the colony. The reluctance of the Georgians to honor Mary's claim infuriated her kinsmen, who recognized her as the oldest living woman in the female line of their clan. Although some Creek factions did not support her, others regarded the actions of the Savannah authorities as another instance of whites using their own rules to bilk Indians of their rightful possessions.

As the controversy simmered, Mary's husband died of illness, and she married again two years later, in 1747, for the third time. Her new husband, an erstwhile Anglican clergyman by the name of Thomas Bosomworth, championed her land claim vigorously, prompting many Georgians to accuse him of high treason. During the summer of 1749, outraged by the protracted negotiations, Bosomworth, Mary, and a body of Creeks, including numerous headmen, marched on Savannah. Outnumbered, the Indians were forced to lay down their arms and surrender. Colonial authorities placed Mary under arrest. But they dared not hold her for long for fear of touching off a larger Indian revolt. She was quickly released and eventually permitted to travel to London with her husband to argue her case before the British Board of Trade.

The dispute dragged on until the summer of 1759 when the British, who were at that time caught up in the last phases of the protracted fighting with the French and their Indian allies for control of North America, offered a compromise. The Crown would put up the islands of Ossabaw and Sapelo for public auction and pay Mary the proceeds. In addition, she would be granted legal possession of Saint Catherines, but only "in consideration of services rendered by her to the province of Georgia," rather than because of any inherent Indian right. Mary accepted the offer. On June 13, 1760, she was presented a deed to the 6,200-acre island, making her the largest landholder in Georgia. But five years later when Mary died, the land passed not to her female relatives, as it would have under the traditions of Creek matrilineage, but to her white husband, Thomas Bosom-

Two Hidatsa women construct a small, tub-shaped craft, known as a bullboat, by stretching the heavy, tough hide of a male buffalo over a willow frame. Used by several Plains tribes to ferry goods down or across rivers, bullboats were made exclusively by women and were light enough to be carried.

worth, based upon English law. Thus the island passed out of Indian hands forever. Today Saint Catherines Island serves as a wildlife preserve.

Many of the cultural changes that came about among the Creek during Mary Musgrove's lifetime had already occurred among the Mohawk of the Northeast when the extraordinary woman known to history as Molly Brant came into the world about 1736. Although the exact place of her birth is unknown, she grew up in the ancient Mohawk village of Canajoharie, a settlement of about 300 people situated 50 miles west of the modern-day city of Schenectady, New York, on the south bank of the river that would later take the name of her people.

By the time Molly was born, the log palisades that once surrounded Canajoharie had long since rotted away. For more than a century, the Mohawk had been yielding land to whites, and they were now almost surrounded by white settlements. Some ancient customs had been lost; others had been altered to fit the new reality. Beset with alcoholism and other diseases, families had withered to the point where they abandoned their famous bark-covered longhouses in favor of small cabins and huts. While the women still planted corn on the flats along the riverbank, many of them also raised chickens and kept a few cows. The residents of Canajoharie and the nearby Mohawk settlement at Fort Hunter still believed in animal spirits and listened to the old stories and legends, but they also attended church on Sundays and had Christian names, dutifully recorded in the baptismal ledgers by Anglican missionaries. Molly's Mohawk name, for example, was Degonwadonti, meaning Several Against One; her baptismal name was Mary (Molly was a nickname).

But even though their glory days were over, the Mohawk were still a force to be reckoned with. The tribe still possessed rich hunting grounds that were coveted by colonial land speculators. And, as keepers of the

eastern door of the mythic Iroquois longhouse, they still had a powerful voice at the Grand Council of the Iroquois, where their representatives and those of the other Iroquois nations—the Oneida, the Tuscarora, the Onondaga, the Cayuga, and the Seneca—decided issues of war and peace. The Six Nations, in turn, strongly influenced the tribes to the west of them, Indians whom they had conquered during the previous century who were a valuable source of pelts for the European fur trade.

The Mohawk social order, if anything, was even more complex than that of the Creek and other eastern tribes. High-ranking clan mothers retained the right to name the Mohawk civil chiefs, or sachems, who presided over local affairs and represented the nation in the Grand Council of the Iroquois League at Onondaga. At the top of the Mohawk elite was the principal sachem of the Turtle Clan bearing the inherited name of Tekarihoga and claiming descent from the first woman on earth.

Unlike Mary Musgrove, Molly Brant was not well connected at birth. Molly's mother, Margaret, a member of the Wolf Clan, had no special rank to pass on to her children. In an earlier era, this lack of high station might have been an insuperable handicap. But in the troubled times of the mid-18th century, the members of great Mohawk families no longer always married within their own class—although they were still required to marry outside their own clan. Thus it happened that after Molly's father died in an epidemic and a subsequent stepfather was killed by enemy Indians, her mother became pregnant by a prestigious sachem from the Turtle Clan named Brant Canagaraduncka, and she eventually married him. By that time, Brant had become a common Mohawk name, and Molly and her younger brother Joseph took it as their surname in the manner of the white people. In the old world of the matrilineal clans, Mohawk children belonged exclusively to the mother, and the father was an outsider. In the new world dominated by Europeans, however, taking the father's name had become a matter of practicality.

With the remarriage of her mother, Molly's prospects for a better life improved dra-

Mandan women land their bullboats near their village, located on a bluff overlooking the Missouri River, in a picture painted by Swiss artist Karl Bodmer in the 1830s. His pencil sketches at left show how the durable little craft was paddled in the water and transported on land.

matically. Her new stepfather, who may have had some Dutch ancestry, was the wealthiest man at Canajoharie. As someone later observed, Brant Canagaraduncka "lived and dressed altogether after the fashion of white men." He owned a prosperous European-style farm and a well-furnished frame house. Brant apparently sent Molly to a British-run school, where she learned to read and write English and developed excellent penmanship. During the years 54 and 1755, he allowed her to accompany him and a delegation of sachems to Philadelphia so that she could witness their discussions with colonial officials about some land transactions.

Most important of all for Molly's future, her stepfather was a great friend of Sir William Johnson, the remarkable Irishman who had come to the Mohawk Valley in 1738 at the age of 23 to serve as an agent for his wealthy uncle, Vice Admiral Sir Peter Warren, a successful trader who owned a large tract of land in the area. Johnson, by all accounts a gregarious and honest man, cultivated the Indians assiduously and soon became a trusted friend, especially of the Mohawks who were his immediate neighbors. He opened up his home to their leaders—including Molly's stepfather—and treated them with dignity and respect. He visited in their huts, wore their clothes, participated in their festivals, and ate their foods. He learned to speak their language and was even able to address them formally, using their own style of colorful oratory. Johnson insisted, for example, that the Mohawk and the British were bound together by an unbreakable silver chain that was fixed to two immovable mountains. The Indians came to accept him as one of their own. They adopted him into the tribe and awarded him the Mohawk name of Warraghiyagey, meaning He Who Does Much Business or A Man Who

Undertakes Great Things. In the early days of the French and Indian War, the British colonial government wisely made Johnson their official representative to the Iroquois and gave him a military commission.

According to Mohawk legend, Molly first caught Johnson's eye during a military muster that was held at his estate. She had gone to the event with her family in order to watch the British display their horses and weapons. A young officer on a particularly spirited horse teasingly invited the young Indian girl to join him for a ride. Much to the officer's surprise, Molly took him up on the offer and sprang onto the saddle behind him. The startled horse took off at high speed and raced around the parade ground, with a laughing Molly clinging to the officer's waist. The spectators thoroughly enjoyed the escapade, especially Johnson.

At the time, Johnson had a common-law wife, a German bond servant by the name of Catherine Weissenberg, with whom he had three children. When Catherine died in the spring of 1759, Johnson invited Molly, who was then about 23 years old, to come live in his household. She soon became pregnant with his child. It was said that they were married in a Mohawk ceremony and much later in the Episcopal church at Fort Hunter, although if a church wedding did take place, all records of the event have been lost. In December 1760, the Canajoharie Mohawks sealed the liaison by presenting Johnson with 80,000 acres of land; he, in turn, presented them with a gift of money. The arrangement created an unshakable bond of friendship between the Mohawks and the energetic Irishman. It was a marriage that would leave its mark on whites and Indians alike. Together the couple had at least nine children, of whom eight—two sons and six daughters—survived infancy. In addition, Molly was also a caring stepmother to Johnson's three oldest children.

Molly was a perfect match for Johnson and proved to be an invaluable asset to his professional life. While he was away on business, Molly ran his large household of slaves and servants—which included several secretaries, a full-time lawyer, a family physician, a blacksmith, a tailor, a gardener, and at least one musician—first at Fort Johnson and later at Johnson Hall, the stately manor house that he built for his growing family in 1763. There she helped him entertain a steady stream of distinguished white and Indian guests. One Englishwoman said of Molly: "Her features are fine and beautiful; her complexion clear and olive-tinted. She was quiet in demeanor, on occasion, and possessed of a calm dignity that bespoke a native pride and consciousness of power. She seldom imposed herself into the picture, but no one was in her presence without being aware of her."

Visitors to Johnson Hall considered "Miss Molly," as she came to be called, the legitimate mistress of the manor; they mentioned her in their thank-you notes to Johnson and sent her personal gifts.

Molly turned out to be an even greater asset to Johnson's backwoods diplomacy. At the time that he began courting her, the British were desperately seeking help from the Iroquois for their war effort against the French. Johnson's marriage to the stepdaughter of a Turtle Clan sachem not only greatly increased his influence among the Indians, it also catapulted the humbly born Molly into a position of enormous prestige. She was now the most powerful woman among the Mohawk. "One word from her," an observer noted, "is more taken notice of by the Five Nations than a thousand from any white man."

This Canadian commemorative stamp, issued in 1986, honors the great 18th-century Mohawk Molly Brant. No known likeness of her exists. The three faces symbolize the many facets of her life and are an idealization, based on a computerized composite made from pictures of her offspring.

Whenever Indians visited Johnson Hall, Molly gave out meals, blankets, clothing, rum, and small gifts of money, in the time-honored manner of a great chief dispensing wealth. Moreover, no colonial official or land speculator could afford to ignore her influence. As one visitor remarked, "When treaties and purchases were about to be made at Johnson Hall, she often persuaded the obstinate chiefs into compliance with the proposals." Throughout the winter and spring of 1765, Molly helped Johnson negotiate a land treaty on the part of the British with the Iroquois and several other western Indian nations. Some 900 Indians subsequently gathered at Johnson Hall to participate in the negotiations. "I have at present every room in my house full of Indians and the prospect before me of continual business all the winter," Johnson wrote.

After her husband's death from illness in 1774, Molly remained loyal to the British cause, as did her brother Joseph, who became the principal Mohawk war leader during the American Revolution. When the Americans confiscated Johnson Hall at the beginning of the war, Molly moved back to Canajoharie, where she continued to encourage the Iroquois to support the Crown. As one of her sons-in-law later recounted, Molly spoke to Cayengwaraghton, the head sachem of the Seneca, "with tears in her eyes," reminding him of her late husband's friendship with her people. She made "other striking arguments and reasonings, which had such an effect upon that chief and the rest of the Five Nations present that they promised her faithfully to stick up strictly to the engagements of her late worthy friend, and for his sake and her sake espouse the king's cause vigorously."

Molly also provided military intelligence to the British, alerting them in 1777, for example, to the location of a contingent of American troops, which the British then successfully ambushed. Her work as a British spy eventually forced her to flee. Once assured of her children's safety, she settled on Carleton Island in the Saint Lawrence River just east of Lake Ontario, where she continued to urge her people to support the British.

The British, however, failed to return the loyalty. When surrendering to the Americans in 1783, they betrayed their Indian friends, signing over control of all lands south of Canada and east of the Mississippi River, including territory that had been reserved for the Iroquois under earlier agreements. Both Molly and her brother Joseph argued strenuously with British officials in an effort to persuade them to vouch for the Iroquois land rights, but to no avail. Stripped of their ancestral holdings, many Iroquois fled to Canada; those who remained behind in the new United States of America found themselves squeezed into increasingly smaller tracts of land and eventually pushed onto reservations.

In recognition of her longstanding services to the Crown, British officials built Molly a home near present-day Kingston, Ontario, and awarded her £1,206 in damages for her lost property in addition to a yearly pension of £100—at

Revered for her modesty, an unmarried Lakota girl named Red Thing That Touches in Marching wears an honorary robe decorated with buttons in this 1832 George Catlin portrait. The geometric designs on her sleeves could be made only by women.

that time the largest compensation ever given to an Indian. Characteristically, she used the money to feed, clothe, and shelter as many of her dispossessed kinspeople as she could. Mindful of her continued influence among the Iroquois, the Americans offered her a sum of money and the opportunity to resettle in her beloved Mohawk Valley. Molly refused. Those offers, "although very great, were rejected with the utmost contempt," reported one of her sons-in-law.

Molly Brant died on April 16, 1796, at the home of one of her daugh-

The designs on the buffalo robe at right, painted by a Cheyenne woman, symbolize the internal organs of a buffalo. It was the task of the women to butcher the animals and distribute the meat and organs.

ters. She was in her 61st year. All of her life, this remarkable woman had identified with her people. Although she was completely at home in the white world, she preferred speaking in Mohawk rather than English and continued to dress in traditional Mohawk frocks, leggings, and moccasins—even though she was accused by her enemies of owning numerous expensive dresses and other luxuries.

Shortly before her death, an anonymous traveler observed a distinguished old lady sitting in a pew at the Episcopal church in Kingston. "We saw an Indian woman, who sat in an honorable place among the English," he recalled. "She appeared very devout during divine service and very attentive to the sermon. She was the relict of the late Sir William Johnson and mother of several children by him, who are married to Englishmen and provided for by the Crown. When Indian embassies arrived, she was sent for, dined at Governor Simcoe's, and treated with respect by himself and his lady." The traveler's words describe a woman who managed to live successfully in two cultures—a woman who took to her grave the steadfast belief that her people could adopt the best of the white man's ways without losing their rich heritage and identity.

About 1738, two years after the birth of Molly Brant, a baby girl was born at the Cherokee town of Chota who would also grow up to become one of the most influential Indian women of the American frontier. Her family named her Nanyehi, meaning One Who Goes About. It was derived from the name of the Spirit People of ancient Cherokee mythology. White settlers later Anglicized it to Nancy. As a girl, Nancy was also called Tsistunagiska, or Cherokee Rose, because, as the legend has it, her skin was as soft as the petals of the wild rose that grows abundantly in the American Southeast.

The Cherokee matrilineal clan system was similar to that of the Creek, and Nancy, like Mary Musgrove, had the advantage of being wellborn. Her mother, Tame Doe, was a member of the Wolf Clan, the largest and one of the most important of the seven Cherokee clans. Tame Doe's brother, Attakullaculla, was Chota's Most Beloved Man, or civil chief. Eight years before Nancy's birth, Attakullaculla made a celebrated trip to London as part of an effort to strengthen trade ties with the British. The identity of Nancy's father is uncertain. Some claim he was a Delaware Indian; others say he was a Cherokee, perhaps even a son of the illustrious Cherokee war chief Oconostota; still others insist he was a British officer named Sir Francis Ward, an uncle of the white trader she later married. Bolstering this view is the fact that Nancy learned to speak English in addition to the dialect of Cherokee that was spoken at Chota.

Chota was one of some 60 Cherokee towns that were grouped along various rivers in the southern Appalachian Mountains. Nancy's birthplace was the principal village of a cluster of settlements known as the Overhill Towns, located on the lower course of the Little Tennessee River and its tributary, the Tellico River, in present-day southern Tennessee. It was famous as a place of refuge, where the shedding of human blood was taboo. Tribal wrongdoers sought sanctuary there until their transgressions were forgiven at the most important event on the Cherokee sacred calendar—the Green Corn Ceremony. This festival marked the death and resurrection of Selu, the Cherokee Mother Corn, and it was held each summer at the ripening of the corn crop.

The Cherokee settlements were far flung: In addition to the Overhill Towns, there were the Lower Towns in the foothills of western South Carolina, along the Keowee and Tugaloo Rivers; the Middle Towns in the mountains of western North Carolina, along the Tuckasegee River and on the headwaters of the Little Tennessee River; and the Valley Towns, along the Hiwassee River, which runs through northern Georgia, southwestern

TAKING UP ARMS WITH MEN

Although fighting was part of the male sphere of activities, Indian women were effective and skillful at it. Usually, the only time they took part was when the men were away from home and they were left behind to defend the elders and children against a surprise enemy attack. In some tribes, however, women traveled with raiding parties as auxiliaries to make camp and cook for the warriors. Stories abound of women who picked up weapons in emergencies and fought alongside the men. Other women went to war to exact revenge for the death of a kinsman or husband. Such a person was Other Magpie, a Crow. After losing a brother to the Sioux, she volunteered as a scout for the U.S. Cavalry. On June 17, 1876—one week before Custer's debacle at the Little Bighorn—Other Magpie, armed with only a knife and a coup stick, took a Sioux scalp during the clash at Rosebud Creek between the forces of General George Crook and Crazy Horse.

A few "manly hearted" women set out from childhood to become warriors. Far from looking down on these fighting women, Indian men honored them, indicating the flexibility of Indian society.

Minnie Hollow Wood, a Sioux, displays a pair of captured saddlebags in a 1927 photograph. For fighting against the U.S. Cavalry, she won the right to wear a war bonnet—a rare honor for a woman.

As a teenager, Elk Hollering in the Water, a Blackfeet, won honors by accompanying her husband on raids against enemy tribes— even though she probably weighed only 100 pounds.

Female Navajo veterans of four wars proudly display a banner celebrating their military service during a 1993 Veterans Day event in Washington, D.C.

North Carolina, and southeastern Tennessee.

Perhaps the isolation of these settlements contributed to the Cherokee's persistent lack of unity, a condition that enabled whites to play one faction off against another. Separate communities rarely cooperated with one another, except in times of crisis, and even then the headmen often acted without regard for the interests of Cherokees living elsewhere. Just as with the Creek, it was the system of matrilineal clans more than anything else that linked the people together. Even so, Cherokee communities tended to go their own way. In the early 1750s, for example, when most Cherokees were seeking peace with their old enemies, the Creek, many Overhills were still feuding with them.

It was during this period of turmoil that Nancy rose to prominence. As was the custom among her people, she married in her teens and quickly gave birth to two children—a son, Fivekiller, and a daughter, Catherine, whose name reflected the English influence on the Cherokee. In 1755 Nancy accompanied her husband, a warrior named Kingfisher, on a raid against a Creek town in northwestern Georgia. When Kingfisher was shot and killed, Nancy picked up his musket and took his place alongside the other warriors. Although warfare was strictly a male domain, Cherokee war parties often brought along a woman to cook and care for their camp—a custom that may explain Nancy's presence on the raid. In any case, her bravery won her great prestige, and upon her return to Chota, the tribal council elected her to the honored position of Ghighau, or Beloved Woman.

Little is known about this female title (which is sometimes translated as Pretty Woman or War Woman), except for the fact that the woman holding it had the final say regarding the fate of prisoners of war. The Beloved Woman could either have the captives put to death by ritual torture or save their lives, in which case she made them her slaves or gave them up for adoption to clans that had lost loved ones. The existence of the title suggests that at some point in their history, the Cherokee may

Medicine Snake Woman, wife of a white trader and daughter of a Blood Indian chief, served in 1853 as a mediator between her people and a party of Americans seeking the most practical route for a railroad linking the Mississippi River and the Pacific Ocean.

have had a formal women's council similar to the council of the men. Although these councils had apparently disappeared by Nancy's time, the women nonetheless exerted enormous influence behind the scenes as advisers and counselors to their brothers, sons, and other male members of their clans, as well as to their own husbands. Indeed, the impact of female lobbying on decision making seemed so pronounced to the well-known 18th-century British trader James Adair that he wryly declared that the Cherokee had a "petticoat government."

Shortly before Nancy became Beloved Woman, Britain and France entered the final phase of their 75-year struggle for dominion over North America. At first the entire Cherokee Nation sided with its principal trading partner, the British. In 1757 Nancy's uncle Attakullaculla invited his allies to establish Fort Loudon on Cherokee land near Chota as part of a line of garrisons to protect the area from attacks by the French and their Indian allies. Several white traders moved to the fort, including a man named Bryant Ward. Although Ward already had a wife who had not yet arrived from Ireland, he courted Nancy. By all accounts, she was a handsome young woman. One observer described her as "tall, erect, and beautiful, with a prominent nose, regular features, clear complexion, long, silken black hair, large, piercing black eyes, and an imperious yet kindly air." Ward also may have been attracted to Nancy because of her influential position. If he married her, he could be assured of the friendship and protection of Attakullaculla and her other powerful male relatives.

Unlike the substantial exchanges of wealth that characterized many Native American weddings, Cherokee marriages involved only the swapping of symbolic gifts. Consequently, Nancy presented Ward with an ear of corn, emblematic of the female realm of horticulture and the main source of Cherokee food; Ward in turn gave her a cut of venison, a sign of the male realm of hunting and a symbol of his promise to provide her with meat. Although Nancy gave birth to a daughter, Elizabeth, by Ward—and possibly a son—he left her as soon as his white wife arrived from Ireland. No one recorded how Nancy felt about her husband's departure, but it probably came as no great shock. Divorces in the Cherokee culture were frequent and easily conducted. The home and the children belonged to the woman and her clan, and a wife could declare that she no longer wanted her husband simply by putting his belongings outside their dwelling. In any case, Nancy and Ward did not sever all ties. Over the years, she and the children occasionally visited him and his white family at his home on the Tugaloo River in South Carolina. A white man who had spent time

THE MOTOKIKS SOCIETY

Women have played important roles in virtually every Native American community, but among the Blackfoot of Canada, they are recognized as the very foundation of the culture. Blackfoot women are the keepers of the most sacred medicine bundles that protect the people's health and well-being. Only they can open the bundles and hand the sacred objects to the men. Only they can evoke the spirits. Without women, no ceremony can take place, including the most sacred of all—the annual Sun Dance.

Long ago, women of the Blood division of the Blackfoot Nation organized the Motokiks, or Old Women's, Society, the female counterpart to the Horn Society, a secret couples association. The primary function of the Motokiks is to acknowledge the importance of the buffalo by paying homage to its spirit. The society has four categories of membership—Birds, Snakes, Bulls, and Scabby Bulls—each possessing its own distinctive regalia. Every summer during the Sun Dance, the Motokiks erect a lodge for ceremonial events to honor the Creator, the buffalo, and the long and storied history of their people.

Wearing sacred robes and headdresses, Bird and Snake members of the Motokiks Society gather on the Blood Indian Reserve in southern Alberta in the 1890s.

A Blackfoot elder named Snake People
Woman wears the headdress of the Scabby
Bulls. All Motokiks carry "iniskims," or
buffalo stones, like the beaded one below.
They possess indescribable power.

Wearing a Bull headdress, an old woman named Maka, or Shorty, holds a bone whistle in her mouth that she blew during ceremonies. The sketches below, made by a Blackfoot woman, show different views of a Bull headdress, including its skirt, which is decorated with four rows of bird feathers.

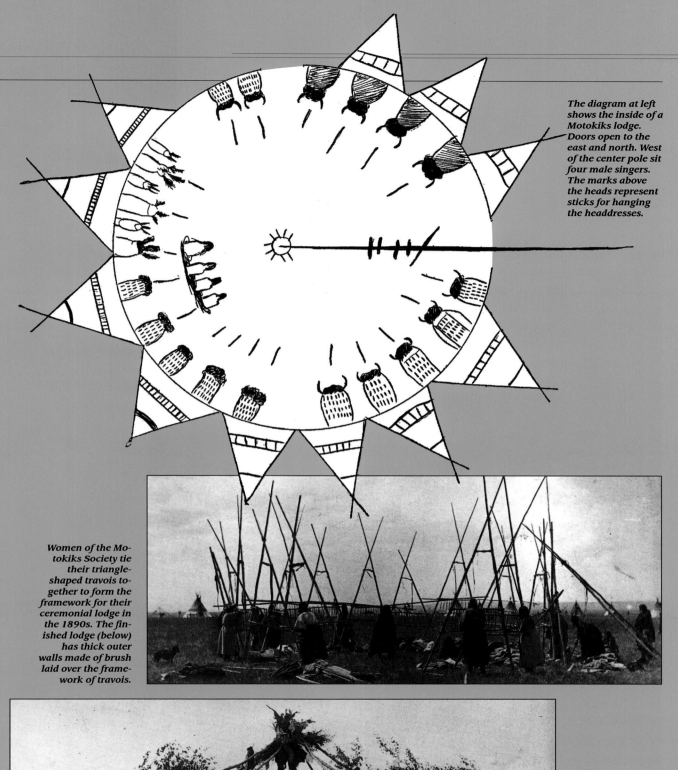

The diagram at left shows the inside of a Motokiks lodge. Doors open to the east and north. West of the center pole sit four male singers. The marks above the heads represent sticks for hanging the headdresses.

Women of the Motokiks Society tie their triangle-shaped travois together to form the framework for their ceremonial lodge in the 1890s. The finished lodge (below) has thick outer walls made of brush laid over the framework of travois.

during his youth with the Wards wrote of meeting Nancy at their home. He described her as "one of the most superior women I ever saw."

The decade of the 1760s was a devastating period for the Cherokee people. Their time-honored alliance with Britain collapsed abruptly when frontiersmen in what is today West Virginia murdered a band of Cherokee warriors in a dispute over the killing of some livestock. The fact that the warriors were returning home after campaigning with the British in the Ohio River valley did not prevent the whites from slaughtering them. The frontiersmen then added insult to injury by trying to collect bounties on the scalps, as if the Cherokees had been hostile Indians. Outraged clansmen of the dead warriors demanded vengeance. Soon, roving bands of Cherokees led by the war chief Oconostota were attacking settlers all across the Carolina and Tennessee frontier. The newly built Fort Loudon was one of the first places to be besieged.

Not all Cherokees approved of the decision to go to war. A number of them had close ties with the settlers. At Fort Loudon, for example, Cherokee women married to white traders and soldiers persisted in smuggling food to their husbands, who had taken refuge within the walls of the garrison. When the war chief Willanaweh threatened the women with death, they mocked him, warning that their clans would retaliate if he dared to harm them. Willanaweh desisted. It is a mark of the temerity of the Cherokee women that at least in this instance they were able to interfere in war operations with impunity.

A wave of violence subsequently engulfed the Cherokee territory. The fighting subsided only after the British had sacked the Lower and Middle Towns, thereby depriving thousands of Indians of food and shelter. By the time Attakulaculla managed to restore peaceful relations with the British late in 1761, perhaps as many as half the population had died—victims either of the fighting or of the famine and the epidemics that followed in its wake. And to make matters worse for the

A 19th-century Mohave girl wears a collar woven of glass beads similar to the one shown below. A sign of wealth, the collars are traditionally burned along with their owners at the time of death.

Indians, the victorious British seized more Cherokee territory as spoils.

Given the tragic outcome of what the British called the Cherokee War, it is not surprising that when the Cherokee found themselves again swept up in a white man's conflict—this time, the American Revolution—they tried to remain neutral. Most Cherokees anticipated a British victory, undoubtedly hoping that the power of the Crown could stem the flood of illegal settlers streaming into Cherokee lands, especially along the Watauga and Holston Rivers. These settlements were in direct violation of a royal decree declaring all land west of the Appalachians reserved for Indians.

In May 1776, a group of Cherokee chiefs gathered in Chota for a council. The British had asked them to attack American settlements near the Watauga River in present-day Tennessee. A young, up-and-coming war chief named Dragging Canoe, who was a son of Oconostota, argued in favor of an immediate attack. Attakullaculla and Oconostota, both old men now, opposed it. Nancy, in her role as Beloved Woman, also spoke out against the attack. It was quite common among the Cherokee for different factions to disagree about matters of war. Even if the majority voted to go to battle, those opposed to the action would not be required to participate. In fact, they could be expected to try to sabotage the attempt, as Nancy did, if they felt it in their group's best interest. As a member of a prosperous faction whose way of life was much more intertwined economically and socially with white society than that of Dragging Canoe and his followers, Nancy knew that she and many other Cherokees had a lot to lose in an all-out war with the Americans. But Dragging Canoe was able to prevail, and several hundred of his warriors painted themselves in preparation for the upcoming battle.

On the night of July 8, Nancy

slipped out of her encampment to free three traders who were being held by Dragging Canoe. She warned them of the impending attack. They, in turn, notified other settlers. Women and children hurried to safety at Fort Caswell, located on the Watauga River north of today's Johnson City, Tennessee, while the men prepared an ambush. In the ensuing battle, 13 Cherokee warriors were killed and many injured, including Dragging Canoe, who was shot in both legs but somehow managed to escape.

Now that the fighting had begun, Nancy did her best to curtail it. Members of Dragging Canoe's faction, however, were bent on seeking revenge against any whites they could lay hands on. One band captured a woman named Mrs. William Bean, who had unwisely ventured out from Fort Caswell to milk the Bean family's cows. The band also held a 12-year-old boy named Samuel Moore. The Indians burned young Samuel at the stake and intended to do the same with Mrs. Bean. But just as they lighted the wood at the woman's feet, Nancy appeared. Waving a swan's-wing charm emblematic of her authority as Beloved Woman, she kicked aside the burning logs and ordered Mrs. Bean freed. Because she had the prerogative of claiming any captive as her slave, Nancy took Mrs. Bean to her home at Chota, where apparently the two women developed a fast friendship. After a few weeks, Nancy released Mrs. Bean and had her escorted back safely to her family.

In the years to come, Nancy interceded to save the lives of more Americans. Yet her efforts to promote peace brought her people little protection. Out of respect for Nancy, Colonel William Christian spared her town of Chota during the brutal campaign to crush Dragging Canoe's resistance in the fall of 1776. It was small consolation, for the Americans also massacred more than 2,000 Cherokee men, women, and children. In 1777 several Cherokee leaders sued for peace and received permission to rebuild their towns. Dragging Canoe's faction, however, remained intractable, moving westward to Chickamauga Creek in northwestern Georgia where they continued to lash out at the whites from their forest hideaways.

In late 1780, Nancy got wind of a new attack on the settlers in the Watauga area. She alerted the Americans and on Christmas Day fed the soldiers camped near Chota with cattle from her

Practicing an ancient form of Native American art, a Cree woman bites a piece of folded birch bark, creating a delicate design similar to the one shown below.

A group of Havasupai girls, dressed for school in calico dresses, sit in a semicircle and play a traditional game.

own herd in the expectation that they would respect the neutrality of her people. But the Americans ignored her pleas. Three days later, they put the torch to Chota and the nearby towns, destroying as many as 1,000 homes and 50,000 bushels of corn that had been stored for the winter. Humiliated and stripped of all her material possessions, Nancy and her family became captives—although they were soon released on orders from Thomas Jefferson, then governor of Virginia.

On July 20, 1781, six months after the outrage at Chota, a group of war-weary Cherokees met with the Americans on the banks of the Holston River in eastern Tennessee to arrange a peace treaty. Much to the surprise of the Americans, the most eloquent speaker among the Indian leaders was a woman—Nancy Ward. "Our cry is all for peace," she proclaimed, "let it continue. This peace must last forever. Let your women's sons be ours; our sons be yours. Let your women hear our words."

Out of respect for the Cherokee Beloved Woman, the American negotiators scaled back their original demands, allowing the Indians more territory than originally intended. But even this small concession was soon lost. The Holston River agreement, like so many others that followed, was broken by the Americans, who wanted, as always, more land. In November 1785, the Cherokees met again with the Americans to settle their disputes. George Washington dispatched a delegation to a site called Hopewell on the Keowee River in South Carolina. The Cherokees sent no fewer than 37 headmen—and their Beloved Woman.

The conference lasted 10 days. Before signing the treaty, which forced them to give up still more land, the Cherokee chiefs asked Nancy, as the symbolic mother of the nation, to address the Americans. The Beloved Woman made a dramatic plea for peace and justice.

"I hope that you have now taken us by the hand in real friendship," she told the white commissioners. "I look on you and the red people as my children. Your having determined on peace is most pleasant to me for I have seen much trouble during the late war. I have borne and raised up warriors. I am old, but hope yet to bear children who will grow up and people our nation as we are now under the protection of Congress and shall have no more disturbance. The talk I have given is from the young warriors I have raised in my town, as well as myself. They rejoice that we have peace, and we hope the chain of friendship will never be broken." At the conclusion of her speech, Nancy presented a string of beads, likening it to the "chain of friendship" that now linked the Indian and white people together. She also brought out a pipe and tobacco, which was lighted and passed around the circle for everyone to smoke.

Although Dragging Canoe and the Chickamauga Cherokees continued their resistance until 1794, the Hopewell Treaty brought peace to Nancy and her people. In the ensuing years, Cherokee culture underwent profound changes. In an effort to survive, the defeated Indians attempted to adopt many of the white man's ways. With many of their hunting grounds taken away from them, Cherokee men turned to farming—hitherto, women's work. Some important headmen even became plantation owners in the manner of the white planters, using

A statue of Nancy Ward, Beloved Woman of the Cherokee people, stands in a Tennessee cemetery over another woman's grave. It remained there for decades, then mysteriously disappeared. Nancy's actual grave is in the southeastern part of the state.

black slaves to work their land. Many Cherokee families attended church and sent their children to school to learn English. Nancy's two daughters both married and settled within the American community. Her sons, however, chose Cherokee wives and settled in Cherokee towns near Chota, where both became headmen.

No matter how much the Cherokee people tried to acculturate, however, the Americans were not satisfied. In May 1817, Cherokee leaders met in council to discuss the adoption of a constitution modeled on that of the United States and to debate the pros and cons of accepting the federal government's offer to relocate the entire Indian nation west of the Mississippi River, where they had been promised a haven. Nancy Ward approved of the new republican form of government but only inasmuch as it provided a means of organizing the people to resist removal from their native soil. Too old and ill to attend the council, Nancy sent her walking stick to indicate her readiness to give up her Beloved Woman title. In addition, she sent a letter that was addressed to the chiefs and warriors and signed by herself and 12 other Cherokee mothers.

"We do not wish to go to an unknown country," the letter states. "We have raised all of you on the land which we now have, which God gave us to inhabit. We have understood some of our children wish to go over the Mississippi, but this act of our children would be like destroying your mothers. Your mothers, your sisters ask and beg of you not to part with any more of our lands. Keep it for our growing children for it was the good will of our creator to place us here."

The approval of the American-style constitution ended the matriarchal clan system and left the Cherokee Nation bitter and divided. In 1819 the tribe sold all of its land north of the Hiwassee River, including Chota. Nancy moved to a plot of land on the Ocoee River near the present town of Benton, Tennessee, where she opened a small inn. There she remained until her death in 1822. She was 84 years old. Sixteen years later, in the winter of 1838-1839, the United States imposed the infamous Trail of Tears migration—the forced removal to the Indian Territory (present-day Oklahoma) that took the lives of perhaps one out of every four Indians. According to legend, Nancy prophesied the coming catastrophe from her deathbed and cried out in anguish at the vision. Upon the expiration of her last breath, her family reported, a white light the color of a swan's wing rose from her body, fluttered around the room, and then flew out the open door like a bird, soaring above the trees in the direction of Chota, the old home of the Cherokee's last Beloved Woman. ◆

A Karok woman stirs a mixture of acorn meal and water heated with stones in a tightly woven basket. Her hat, fashioned in the shape of an acorn cap, is an indication of wealth.

RECEIVING NATURE'S BOUNTY

For as long as anyone can remember, the ritual gathering and preparation of wild plants has been in large part the domain of Native American women. Each Indian culture observes its own traditional harvest season, employs its own sacred implements to perform the work, and celebrates the gifts of life from Mother Earth by incorporating them into their own unique ceremonies that typically celebrate the renewal and regeneration of the world and its people.

The practice of acorn gathering by the Indians of California continues to this day—even though some of the Indians have been displaced from their original homelands. Each year, they return to the oak groves to gather acorns from ancestral trees passed down through the generations. Men and boys set to work with long sticks, knocking the smaller, acorn-laden branches to the ground. But the responsibility for gathering and preparing this food is reserved traditionally for the women. From an early age, Indian girls are still taught the lore of the acorn, thought by the Pomo to have been planted by the culture hero Bluejay, who wanted to ensure enough acorns for himself to eat. Women are responsible for transforming the nuts into a finely pounded meal that can be used to make nourishing dishes. Young girls are trained by their mothers to treat the acorn with respect and to honor its bounty by observing age-old traditions. The Hupa, for example, sanctify the first eating of the acorns each fall with a special feast that ensures the continuing supply of this nutritious food. After the first nuts are gathered and ritually cooked, lengthy prayers and other sacred acts are performed. Only then are the people permitted to consume the nuts.

The sequence above shows how acorns are prepared. After being leached to remove tannic acid, the nuts are shelled and then pounded into meal with a stone pestle and flat mortar. Next, the flour is sifted. The larger pieces are separated out and pounded again. Water, heated by hot stones, is then mixed with the meal. The mixture is cooked into a mush that can be either diluted with water to make soup or baked into biscuits or bread.

Northwest California men perform the White Deerskin Dance, a part of the World Renewal Ceremony. Held every other year, usually in the fall, the ceremony gives thanks to the Creator for sharing acorns and other earthly riches.

Photographed in 1906, an Apache woman uproots a mescal crown with a stick and a stone (top left). Trimmed crowns are stacked by the roasting pit (left) ready to be covered with brush and topped with dirt. The mescal usually cooks for several days.

THE GIFT OF THE MESCAL

The Mescalero Apache were so named by the Spaniards because of their practice of eating mescal, a type of agave, or century plant. Traditionally, the Mescalero disdained the eating of fish and most fowl, making mescal a dietary necessity. While no longer a staple, mescal continues to be consumed and treated with the same reverence. In the late spring, Mescaleros still travel to the higher elevations where the women harvest the plant. Using a sharp, pointed stick and a hatchetlike knife, they pry up the crown of the plant and trim it. The men build wide, shallow cooking pits that serve as ovens.

Prayers and rituals accompany each step of the process. Experienced women supervise the cooking, exercising great care to follow proper procedures in order to ensure bountiful future harvests. They first roast the mescal, then cut up the hearts for immediate consumption. The bases of the leaves are sun dried and made into cakes, which are distributed to the people.

A worker in Carlsbad, New Mexico, throws brush into a pit full of mescal crowns in preparation for roasting. The women shown at right are preparing the cooked mescal for eating.

In a life-giving blessing ritual connected with numerous Apache ceremonies, including the Mescal Roast, a painted dancer performs the Mountain Spirit Dance. The Mountain Spirit People are credited with bringing agriculture to the Apache.

Two Crow women pick buffalo berries in a thicket in this archival photograph. The berries were carried back to camp in uniformly sized burden baskets that helped measure the quantity of the harvest.

BERRY PICKING ON THE GREAT PLAINS

The Plains Indians supplemented their basic diet of buffalo meat with a variety of wild berries. Picking season began in late spring and continued throughout the summer. Berry picking has always been associated with the communal buffalo hunt and the annual life-giving ceremony of the Sun Dance.

Berrying was both a sacred ritual and a social activity; groups of women picked together, gossiping, reminiscing, and enjoying each other's company, but always showing a proper reverence for the fruit. This was also one of the few times of the year when a young man could court his sweetheart.

The berries were an essential ingredient of pemmican, a winter staple for many tribes. It usually consisted of dried buffalo meat (today, deer or antelope is often substituted) that had been pounded to a powder and mixed with melted fat, marrow, and crushed berries.

A buffalo skull hangs from the center pole of a Sun Dance lodge during the annual ceremony that allows the people to renew their lives by means of pledges, purifications, and other sacred rituals. Berries are also an integral part of this ritual.

A modern-day Crow woman picks berries on the Crow Reservation in southern Montana (opposite, far left). Her partner at left is shown culling the berries before processing them into foodstuffs.

With a carrying bag slung about her waist, a Yakima woman digs up the earth with a root stick in this Edward Curtis photograph. Although agriculture was part of the female domain, the root sticks used were made by men.

EARTH'S HIDDEN TREASURES

For centuries, Plateau Indians living in what are today parts of Washington State and Oregon have celebrated spring by gathering nourishing roots from the fields along the Columbia River flood plain. At the arrival of the new season, communities appoint respected female elders as ceremonial root diggers to bring in the first harvest.

Accompanying their work with prayers and songs, the women return to their villages to boil the roots in prepa-

ration for the first food feast, a widespread observance that was commonly practiced at the beginning of every gathering season. The celebration assured the people of the continuation of the edible root-producing plants. Only after giving appropriate thanks and partaking of the first food are the village families free to collect their own roots. A skilled woman might dig up as many as 60 bushels of roots for her family during the short gathering season.

To the beat of male drummers, women in Priest Rapids, Washington, participate in their community's first food ceremony in 1951.

The photographs at far left show women on the Warm Springs Reservation in Oregon harvesting roots in the traditional manner. After digging them up with root sticks and collecting them in bags, the group celebrates (left) with prayers directed by a male bell ringer.

Maricopa fruit pickers stand beside a giant saguaro cactus in this Edward Curtis photograph. They carry the fruit in baskets, balanced on their heads; when empty, the baskets serve as sun hats.

THE SAGUARO'S RITUAL WINE

The Papago Indians of the Sonoran Desert region mark their new year with the harvest of fruit from the towering saguaro cactus, a plant that can grow to heights of 50 feet or more. In late June or July, women led by a grandmother go into the desert with long poles to pluck mature fruit from high atop the cactus. The women scoop the fruit into baskets, taking care to leave the empty pods faceup on the ground so that the spirits will send rain. After the fruit is boiled in water, it is strained and cooked some more to yield a thick red syrup that the women seal in earthen jars, called *ollas,* and store in the village roundhouse, also known as the rain house. There the community patriarch performs secret rites allowing the wine-maker to transform the juice into wine.

When it is ready a few days later, the villagers gather outside the rain house for the rainmaking ceremony. Ritual wine is presented to the elders, then to the people who stand encircling them. Songs asking for the blessings of rain invariably usher in the rainy season.

A line of 13 male and female dancers perform their steps beside jars of wine, picking
poles, and two fires in a painting entitled
"Rain House and Saguaro Wine Festival"
by the Papago artist Michael Chiago.

A woman rakes fruit from a towering cactus
(far left) with a long picking pole. Encased
in a flowerlike pod, the bright red saguaro
fruit is the size of a hen's egg (center, left).
Before it is boiled, the fruit must be removed from its pod (center, right). Vats of
saguaro fruit (left) cook over mesquite fires.

3

Keeping ancient customs alive, women of New Mexico's Santa Clara Pueblo ceremonially grind kernels of corn during one of the village's most important yearly festivals, the Corn Grinding Dance. Indians of the Southwest have used rough stones called metates, such as the ones shown at top, to make cornmeal since before the Spaniards conquered their land in the 16th century.

KEEPERS OF THE FAITH

On a July night in 1958, nearly 100 Kashaya Pomos gathered in their dance house at Stewarts Point, California, for a ceremony that reflected both their commitment to tradition and their capacity to adapt. The Kashaya dance house—a windowless wooden building with a tunnel-like entryway, a fireplace, and plank benches set around the perimeter of a dirt floor—was similar to those in which native Californians of various tribes had long assembled to commune with the spirits that sustained them. On this occasion, as in earlier times, the ceremony included a stirring performance by dancers wearing magnificent feathered headdresses called Big Heads. To the rhythmic strains of singers, four Big Head Dancers circled around the fire, shaking so vigorously that, from time to time, long plumes came loose from their caps and fell to the floor, where they were retrieved by an attendant.

Over the centuries, dancers such as these had been delighting and inspiring Native American onlookers, who saw in them an embodiment of the bountiful spirits. In one important respect, however, this ceremony marked a departure from tradition. In other times and places, it was only men who were entitled to don the majestic headdresses and personify the spirits. Here among the Kashayas, all the Big Head Dancers were women, as was the leader of the ceremony—a *maru,* or "dreamer," whose visions and teachings not only inspired such rituals but also guided the religious life of the community as a whole.

This honored dreamer was named Essie Parrish, and for the preceding 15 years, she had served as prophet, or spiritual leader, of the Kashaya Pomos. She was the second woman in succession to fill that role for the community since the late 1800s—a time of wrenching change for the dwindling Kashayas, whose numbers were reduced to little more than 100 by the early 20th century.

One of many branches of the diverse Pomo tribal group, the Kashayas had long flourished in their homeland along the Sonoma coast by making extended forays from their villages to harvest acorns from hillside oak groves, draw fish from the fog-shrouded bays and streams, and gather reeds and bark for their dwellings from the tule marshes and dense redwood forests. In the mid-19th century, however, white ranchers began to claim the territory of the Kashayas and hem them in. Peaceful by nature, they were left with little choice but to live as tenants on the newly established ranches, where they picked crops and performed domestic chores for subsistence wages. Demoralized by the changes in their way of life, the Kashayas sought reassurance in a new spiritual movement that harmonized with their traditional beliefs. It was no accident that women came to play a leading role in this movement, for they had long served the community as healers and as guardians of tribal traditions. Essie Parrish herself was an accomplished healer, weaver, and storyteller as well as the mother of 15 children. Among the Kashayas as among other Indian groups under stress, such capable women were called upon to help restore the faith and resolve of their people, while men continued to figure prominently in tribal affairs.

The spiritual movement of which Essie Parrish served as maru had its roots in the traditional rites performed among the tribes of central California by elaborately costumed dancers of the sacred Kuksu Society. In the early 1870s, a new ceremony reached the troubled Kashayas from the Paiutes of Nevada—the Ghost Dance, whose adherents believed that white people and their world would soon be destroyed but that Indians who joined in the dance would be saved and reunited with their departed ancestors. The Kashayas and others in the region gathered in subterranean dance houses in anticipation of that great event. Enthusiasm soon faded when the day of reckoning failed to occur, but the maru and her followers continued to believe that sacred dancing and other native traditions offered them spiritual protection in an uncertain world.

Essie Parrish entered that world in 1902, growing up on a ranch that was owned by a white settler. She was raised largely by her maternal grandmother, a woman steeped in tribal lore who enchanted the young girl with tales from the past. More than other Kashaya children of her time, Parrish heeded those stories, replete with haunting images of supernatural creatures and warnings of the afflictions that befell those who broke ancestral taboos. Eagerly, Parrish absorbed the lessons of her grandmother and other elders in the tribe. "I used to like to be around the old people," she later remembered. "They used to talk of the old ways, and it really interested me." While she was still a child, Parrish also applied herself to mastering traditional skills and crafts, particularly the weaving of baskets. From an aunt, she learned to tend and gather the requisite grasses and roots and fashion them into finely woven vessels.

Kashaya Pomo spiritual leader Essie Parrish wears a huge feathered headdress and holds two bead-decorated staffs for a ceremony she presided over in 1958, with the assistance of the woman beside her. Prime organizer of the rituals held in the dance house at Stewarts Point, Essie Parrish was also renowned as a healer and prophet.

But the special powers that distinguished Essie Parrish as a healer and prophet came not from the lessons of her elders but from visions that put her in touch with the spirit world early in life. One fateful encounter occurred when she was only six years old. Parrish was walking home through the woods when she glimpsed a *walepu*—a frightful creature with a human face and a cloak of many feathers, who could sing like the birds and cause sickness or even death. Terrified, Parrish limped home, where she fell into a stupor. No one was able to rouse her, until a man who himself claimed the powers of a walepu and knew how to counter the creature's spells was called in. The man sang over Parrish's inert body until she at last regained consciousness.

Several years later, at the age of 11, she acquired her own special song in a dream. "As I lay asleep," she recalled as an adult, "I heard singing up in the sky." The song came to her from a man high above her, and she could feel it enter deep into her chest: "After I awoke from sleep, that song was singing inside me all day long. Even though I didn't want to sing, still the song was singing in my voice box. Then I myself tried, tried to sing, and amazingly the song turned out to be beautiful. I have remembered it ever since." About two years later, her younger sister fell ill, and Parrish was called upon by a relative to cure her. She prayed to heaven and laid her

DESERT CAHUILLA
MEDICINE WOMAN

MEDICINE WOMEN

Of all the female roles in Native American cultures, perhaps none is as powerful as that of medicine woman. Like her male counterpart, a medicine woman, or shaman, is considered to have a special connection to the spirit world that can be used either for good or for evil. This link, which often comes initially through a dream or vision, is what empowers her to heal. And, since physical and emotional afflictions are believed to reflect an imbalance between the natural world and the spirit world, or human contact with an evil influence, a medicine woman's task is to restore harmony and balance.

Some medicine women dispense herbs or poultices as part of their healing, while others rely on spoken formulas—or literally suck the evil out of their patients; in several tribes, in fact, only women can use the sucking remedy. But nearly all healers invoke the aid of a "dream helper," an ally from the spirit world who appears in order to guide the healer. The helper may be a bear, hummingbird, badger, or other animal; a Desert Cahuilla medicine woman was helped by a spirit named Ahswit, or Eagle, for example, while a Crow healer called upon ants for assistance.

Medicine women assume this role either by design or by fate—and sometimes by a little of both. Many women learn the tools of the trade by watching their grandparents, parents, or other family members, gaining practical knowledge that is passed down from one generation to the next. Others seek training from established shamans in their communities.

Even the best instruction, however, is sometimes not enough to make a woman a healer. Especially in the nonherbal realm, that status can come only after she has been in touch with the spirit world through a dream. In a number of tribes, that does not happen until after menopause. But in others, such as the Navajo, young women entering puberty are seen as especially ripe for the honor. In any case, the power to heal usually remains with the woman until her death, which is a cause for great sorrow among her people.

CHEROKEE MEDICINE
WOMAN AND CHILD

KIOWA MEDICINE WOMAN

PIEGAN MEDICINE
WOMAN

HUPA SHAMAN

REMEDIES FOR THE AILING

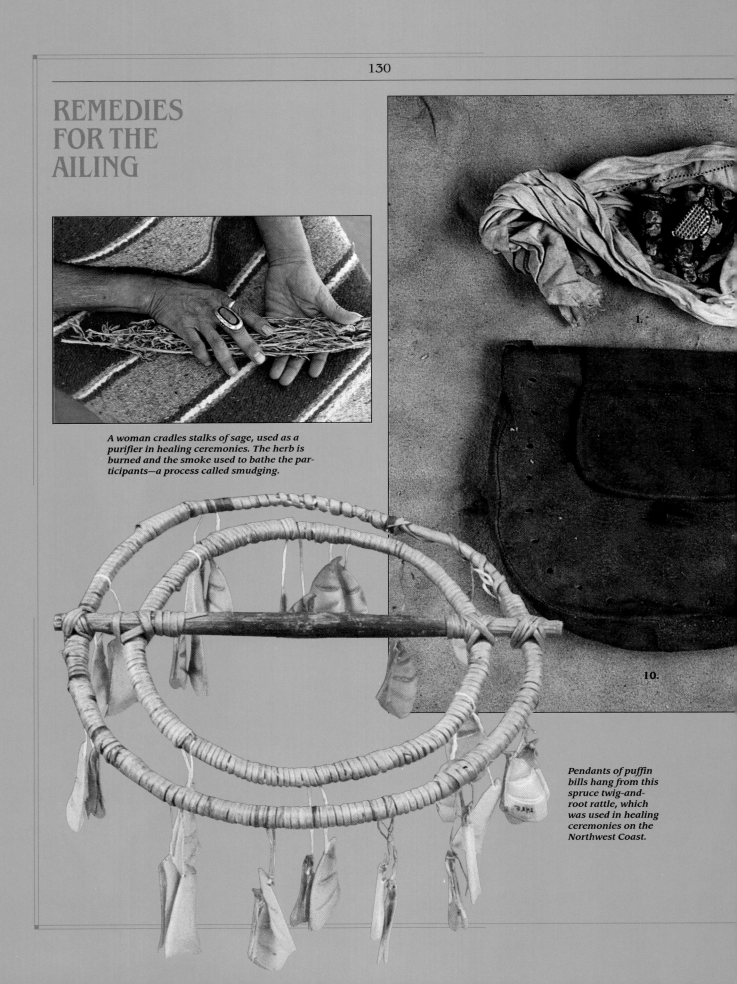

A woman cradles stalks of sage, used as a purifier in healing ceremonies. The herb is burned and the smoke used to bathe the participants—a process called smudging.

1.

10.

Pendants of puffin bills hang from this spruce twig-and-root rattle, which was used in healing ceremonies on the Northwest Coast.

Every medicine woman had her own remedies for ailments; this medicine kit was carried by a Blackfeet healer.

1. INDIAN TURNIP (FOR GAS)
2. LOBELIA SEEDS (FOR VENEREAL DISEASE)
3. MUSKRAT ROOT (FOR SORE THROATS)
4. WILD RHUBARB (MILD CATHARTIC)
5. SNAKEROOT (FOR SNAKEBITE)
6. TRILLIUM (FOR FEMALE AND HEART PROBLEMS)
7. SUMAC ROOT (FOR HEMORRHOIDS AND TOOTHACHES)
8. JUNIPER (TO INCREASE FLOW OF URINE)
9. WILD GERANIUM (AN ASTRINGENT)
10. BUCKSKIN CARRYING BAG

These healing implements may have been used by a Crow medicine woman: The stomach kneader (right, bottom) helped to relieve indigestion, while the sucking tube (right) was used to extract the evil spirits causing the illness.

PRACTICING THE POWER TO HEAL

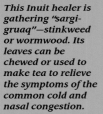

This Inuit healer is gathering "sargi-gruaq"—stinkweed or wormwood. Its leaves can be chewed or used to make tea to relieve the symptoms of the common cold and nasal congestion.

"The plants call me and let me know where they are and how I can use them for my medicines and my dyes," says Katie Henio, a shepherdess on the Ramah Navajo Reservation in New Mexico, shown in the pictures at right gathering herbs and preparing a poultice.

Having been "molded" by older aunts during her own puberty ceremony, a young Navajo woman is now empowered to do the same. She is helping to shape this young girl into maturity.

Clad in buckskin, a Sioux medicine woman, who is both a skilled herbalist and a spiritual assistant, participates in a Sun Dance procession on the Pine Ridge Reservation in South Dakota.

right hand on her sister's head. Then a new song with healing power came to her: "I didn't sing it out loud; it was singing down inside of me. 'I wonder how I am going to cure her,' I was thinking to myself. To my amazement she got well a few days afterward. That was the first person I cured."

Over the years, Essie Parrish's reputation as a healer increased. By the time she was 18, she knew that curing people was to be her mission in life. The power that had first come to her in the form of a song entered her hands and her throat, and she found that she could make people better by touching them and by putting her mouth to the afflicted part of their body and drawing out the illness—a sucking ritual that was practiced by healers among a number of Native American peoples. "Here, somewhere in the throat, the power sits," Parrish explained later. Such were her doctoring skills that they were in demand not only among the Kashayas but also among neighboring peoples.

While Essie Parrish was still developing her gifts as a young woman, the spiritual leader of the Kashayas was Annie Jarvis, a resolute woman who urged her people to keep their culture intact by forswearing drinking and gambling and by avoiding contact with the white world. Jarvis barred her followers from marrying non-Indians and from sending their children away to the boarding schools that white authorities had established to promote the assimilation of young Indians into the larger society. Shortly before she died, Jarvis entrusted her leadership responsibilities to Essie Parrish, who served as prophet from 1943 until her own death in 1979. During that time, Parrish turned away from the isolationism of her predecessor. Although profoundly attached to Kashaya traditions, she believed that her people could derive inspiration from the outside world as well. Like a number of her followers, she embraced Mormonism without yielding in her devotion to the sacred dances and other native rituals. She came to attribute her healing gifts to a single supreme spirit. "That's my power," she declared, "the one I call Our Father."

As a part of her openness, Parrish welcomed members of the white community who were interested in preserving knowledge of Kashaya ways. It was at her invitation that anthropologists witnessed the dance house ceremony in 1958. She also participated in the making of more than two dozen films illustrating various aspects of her culture; shared her knowledge of weaving and basketry with museum curators; and worked with linguist Robert Oswalt of the University of California to compile a Kashaya dictionary and a collection of tribal legends, songs, and reminiscences, which were transcribed both in Kashaya and in English.

Photographed in 1910, Ira Henry of California's Yurok tribe wears a woven cap of the sort Indian women of the region long crafted with consummate artistry and devotion. The example above was made of strips of hazel, willow, pine root, bear grass, and fern.

Nevertheless, Parrish made her greatest contribution to her people as their maru, the leader whose dreams uplifted them and shaped their ceremonies. A number of the songs chanted during the rituals and the costumes worn by the dancers were inspired by her visions. Nowhere was her influence more apparent, however, than in the unique form that the Big Head Dance took among the Kashaya people. According to tradition, the men who performed that dance renewed the world by impersonating bountiful spirits, who then responded to the rousing ceremony by showering the people with blessings. Essie Parrish, who had done a great deal to restore the hopes of the Kashayas, knew that women were needed to renew the world, and consequently, she reserved the dance for them.

Parrish's story echoes that of other determined Native American women who drew on tribal traditions to cope with the challenges of the 20th century. Some served as healers or spiritual guides. Others sought to revive or reinterpret ancient crafts such as pottery, both as a means of supporting their kin and as a way of keeping faith with the past. Still others worked to preserve the oral traditions by passing down important stories and legends. And, especially in recent times, many have expanded on the traditional influence exerted by Indian women over families, clans, and councils and emerged as tribal leaders, helping to defend the ancestral rights of their people.

In their various capacities, all these women have had to confront the bitter legacy of the 19th century, when native peoples were deprived of their autonomy and treated as if they had no culture worth preserving. Most tribal groups were confined to reservations, where the federal government subjected them to a bewildering array of programs aimed at eradicating their native customs and converting them to modern American ways. As it turned out, the lands set aside for Indians were often mar-

Carrying baskets and wearing ornate headdresses, dancers from San Juan Pueblo perform the traditional Basket Dance during a 1974 festival of New Mexico Indians. The winter dance, intended to bring spring rains so crops will flourish, remains unchanged from the ancient ceremony depicted in the painting at far left.

ginal, and lacking the necessary capital from the government for large-scale farming, many men abandoned the plow in disappointment and sought other employment. Meanwhile, women on some reservations continued as they had in the past to wield their hoes and rakes and tend small gardens that helped sustain their families.

Among those who helped preserve the craft and lore of gardening was the Hidatsa Buffalo Bird Woman, who continued to cultivate corn and other crops with notable success long after the government relocated her tribe to North Dakota's Fort Berthold Reservation in 1882 and promoted farming there by the men. Buffalo Bird Woman was a member of the Hidatsa Goose Society, a group of women who presided over the gardens and performed ceremonies designed to promote growth. Among other tribes, there were many similar organizations associated with activities and rituals that had long been entrusted to women. Some of those societies endured when tribes were confined to reservations, while others languished, only to be revived in the 20th century by Indian women who were intent on reclaiming their heritage.

The survival of the women's societies was just one aspect of a larger phenomenon—the adherence of reservation dwellers to tribal customs that were often actively opposed by white authorities. In 1883, for example, Commissioner of Indian Affairs Hiram Price issued a directive that established courts on the reservations to discourage what he called "the demoralizing influence of heathenish rites." Among the practices punishable by the courts were the activities of shamans and solemn ceremonies such as the Sun Dance, during which worshipers endured privation and suffering as a test of their devotion to the spirits. Women played a part in this ritual and in other outlawed practices, and many of them kept faith with the old ways. Along with their menfolk, they perpetuated their sacred observances through secrecy, evasion, and outright defiance. In the 1930s, the ban on the Sun Dance was finally lifted, and other forms of native religious expression emerged from the shadows as well.

Another aspect of federal policy that deeply affected the lives of Indian women was the effort to assimilate reservation dwellers into the mainstream culture through education. To that end, the government established dozens of agency schools on reservations and about 20 boarding schools off the reservations. In 1879 the first government academy for boarders, the Carlisle Indian School, opened its doors in Pennsylvania to 82 Sioux, Pawnee, and Kiowa students. Over the next two decades, more than 1,200 Indian students from 79 different tribes attended Carlisle alone.

Arikara women at Fort Berthold Reservation in North Dakota carry bundles of brush to be used in making a lodge for a ceremonial dance performed about 1900. Women helped preserve such observances on reservations in spite of opposition from federal Indian agents.

There, boys were expected to care for the institution's dairy barns, while girls were charged with sewing school uniforms—tight, heavy garments with high collars and long rows of buttons down the front, unlike anything the children had worn at home. Youngsters at the boarding schools were subject to beatings if they lapsed into their native tongue. One student, Helen Sekaquaptewa of the Hopi, recalled her experiences: "Evenings we would gather and cry softly so the matron would not hear and scold or spank us," she wrote. "I can still hear the plaintive little voices saying, 'I want to go home. I want my mother.' "

For some girls, however, boarding school served as a source of strength in ways the government never envisioned. Amid the harsh treatment they sometimes received at the hands of their teachers and the stress they often felt at having to conform to an alien culture, the students established enduring friendships with one another—relationships that often crossed tribal lines and formed a foundation for the pan-Indian movement that took hold in later years. Students did acquire skills that were useful in the larger society, but they remained keenly aware of the ways in which whites set Indians apart and belittled their culture. Many of the women who were educated by the government used the knowledge they acquired not to immerse themselves in the mainstream but to serve their own people and fight for the rights of Indians as a whole.

Susan La Flesche, the daughter of an Omaha chief, attended Virginia's Hampton Normal and Agricultural Institute, founded as a boarding school for young blacks after the Civil War but opened up to include a group of Indians in 1878. After graduation she went on to study at the Women's Medical College in Philadelphia and become the first Indian woman to be licensed as a physician in the United States. Far from neglecting her heritage, La Flesche devoted the remainder of her life to practicing medicine on the Omaha reservation located along the Missouri River in Nebraska. The job was demanding, both physically and emotionally. Many of the 1,200 tribal members were skeptical of nontraditional medicine. In order to reach the most desperately ill, La Flesche had to travel over rough and rutted roads that were nearly impassable in bad weather. Each night she kept a lighted lamp in the front window of her home as a beacon to let the sick know that a doctor was on call.

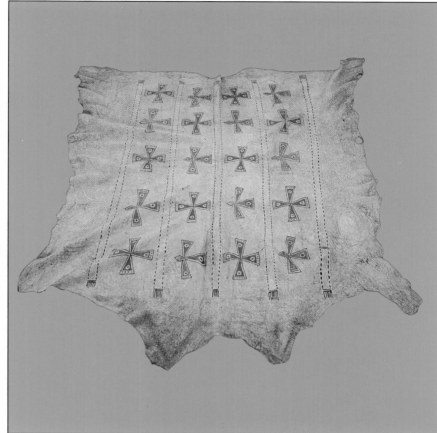

Vibrantly dressed Lakota Sioux women take part in the Sun Dance, a sacred ritual still practiced by Plains tribes to celebrate the coming of summer. An elkhide Sun Dance robe (above, right), adorned with crosses representing the butterfly, bringer of dreams, was worn by a Blackfeet holy woman in the 1840s.

Susan's older sister Susette gained fame as a crusader for Indian rights. When Susette was born in 1854, the La Flesche family (the name came from the girls' grandfather, a French trapper) still lived in a traditional Omaha earth lodge and took part in buffalo hunts. As soon as she could walk, Susette was initiated into the tribe during a Turning the Child ritual at which she received her Indian name—Inshta Theumba, or Bright Eyes. By the time her sister Susan was born in 1865, however, the Omaha way of life had largely disappeared. The family now lived in a two-story frame house, and many Omaha men had abandoned hunting and taken up farming in the manner of whites.

Susette La Flesche attended the mission school on the reservation until a loss of government funds caused it to close temporarily. With the help of a former teacher, she transferred to the fashionable Elizabeth Institute for Young Ladies in New Jersey. After graduating in 1875, she returned

home to teach Indian children. She enjoyed her work and might have remained in the teaching profession if not for the dramatic trial of the Ponca chief Standing Bear in April 1879. Susette's involvement in that landmark case changed her life.

The Ponca, a neighboring tribe closely related to the Omaha, had been relocated against their will from their rich homeland along the Niobrara River in Nebraska to an infertile tract in the Indian Territory (Oklahoma). The Ponca suffered terribly. During the first years after removal, as many as one-fourth of their number died of starvation and disease. Among the dead was Standing Bear's son. Before he died, the boy begged his father to bury him beside his sister in their old Nebraska homeland, and Standing Bear set out to honor the request. But when white settlers saw the Ponca funeral procession crossing lands that had been supposedly cleared of all Indians, they feared an uprising and notified the army. A detachment of cavalry arrested Standing Bear and put him and his followers in prison.

Girls of the first class to attend Pennsylvania's Carlisle Indian School—most still wearing blankets and other native garb—line up for a group portrait in 1879. Many of these students, homesick and subjected to harsh discipline, returned to their reservations before graduating.

Standing Bear's plight attracted the attention of Thomas Henry Tibbles, an editor for the *Omaha Herald.* Tibbles wrote a series of sympathetic articles publicizing the case. As a result, two lawyers volunteered to help the Ponca people and promptly issued a writ of habeas corpus, a legal claim against imprisonment without just cause. Government lawyers countered that "an Indian is not a person" and thus could not make use of such a writ. Judge Elmer S. Dundy, however, ruled against the government, saying that the Indians were equal under the law and that there was no authority to force them back to the Indian Territory.

Susette La Flesche had relatives living among the Ponca and had witnessed their suffering firsthand. At the request of Tibbles, she made a fact-

finding trip to the Indian Territory to gather evidence to help the tribe regain its former lands. Afterward, she made an impassioned presentation of her findings to a committee of government officials. Recognizing her effectiveness as a public speaker, Tibbles arranged for La Flesche and her half brother Francis, who later became a noted anthropologist, to accompany Standing Bear on a tour of eastern cities to win public sympathy for the Indians. In March 1881, in no small part because of La Flesche's testimony before Congress, the federal government granted the Ponca a reservation along the Niobrara River.

La Flesche eventually married Tibbles, and the pair traveled around the country, lecturing and lobbying for Indian reform, particularly for the right of Native Americans to become full citizens. Her speeches and writings rallied many influential whites to the Indian cause, including the poet

Henry Wadsworth Longfellow and Helen Hunt Jackson, author of a famous exposé of the U.S. government's treatment of the Indians, published in 1881. Susette La Flesche also inspired the founding of several major Indian reform groups, including the Women's National Indian Association and the Boston Indian Citizenship Committee.

Other Indian women who came to the attention of the outside world served as interpreters of their culture, instilling in whites an appreciation for Native American traditions. One such interpreter who won renown about the turn of the 20th century was writer and orator Pauline Johnson. The offspring of a mixed couple, a Mohawk chief and the daughter of a white missionary at the Six Nations Reservation in Canada, Johnson profited by her ancestry to appeal to white audiences and convey to them the richness of her Indian inheritance.

Even though her skills as a speaker and her partly Western background enabled her to move freely among fashionable elements of Canadian and English society, she always defined herself as a Mohawk. "There are those who think they pay me a compliment by saying I am just like a white woman," she told an acquaintance. "I am Indian, and my aim, my joy, and my pride is to sing the glories of my own people." She did so in verse and in stories, which she frequently recited from the stage, wearing a costume of her own design, including a buckskin dress, leggings, and moccasins. Billed as the Mohawk Princess, she presented a romantic image to the public, but her devotion to her native heritage was genuine and left a deep impression on her audiences.

For all the attention that was paid to women like Pauline Johnson who interpreted Indian ways to the white population, the task of preserving tribal cultures was shouldered in large part by those who remained close to their communities and worked in relative anonymity. Although educating whites about Indians was sometimes included in their mission, they were primarily concerned with rekindling the ancestral fires of hope and inspiration within their own circles. For only by the light of tradition, they believed, would their people be able to emerge from the darkness that had befallen them in recent times and move forward.

Among the Indian women who brought the lessons of the past to bear on the problems afflicting Native Americans in the 20th century was the Comanche healer Sanapia, who by the time she matured as a medicine woman in the 1940s

Examples of exquisite workmanship, the dance stick at right was decorated with beadwork by Claire Packard of South Dakota's Yankton Sioux in 1992, and the box at left was crafted of birch bark and dyed porcupine quills by an Ottawa artisan in northern Michigan in 1972.

was the tribe's sole surviving eagle doctor—a shaman who claimed power from that revered bird. Born in 1895 at Fort Sill, Oklahoma, Sanapia was the product of a marriage that reflected the deep tensions between the traditional beliefs of the Comanches on the reservation—who had been confined there with much reluctance and resistance—and the values impressed on them by white missionaries and government agents. Sanapia's father adopted Christianity and European-style dress and encouraged his daughter to act in a way that would win approval from whites. Her mother, on the other hand, was a staunch traditionalist who knew English but declined to speak it in public so long as whites remained ignorant of her native tongue. On one occasion, young Sanapia returned from the mission day school she attended wearing button-top shoes she had received there. Her mother warned her that the shoes would cripple her, but her father insisted that she keep them on. When the shoes began to hurt her feet, Sanapia heeded her mother and did without them.

In the years to come, Sanapia's mother influenced her in more significant ways. After students at the mission school were invited to enroll in a federal boarding school in Kansas, her brothers were sent there, but her mother refused to allow Sanapia to join them on the grounds that she would not be safe. By keeping Sanapia close to home, her mother also ensured that the girl would remain in touch with traditions that the mother's side of the family cherished and hoped to perpetuate. Both Sanapia's mother and her maternal uncle were eagle doctors. And among those urging Sanapia to follow that healing path was her maternal grandmother, who lived in a tipi outside her parents' house and steeped the young Sanapia in tribal lore. "She's the one who told me to take my mother's doctoring-way," Sanapia explained later. "My grandmother said that soon in the future there wouldn't be hardly any Indian doctors left." At the age of 14, Sanapia left school and embarked on her apprenticeship as a healer.

For the next four years, Sanapia spent much of her time with her mother and uncle, studying their craft. She learned to identify and apply the many plants and herbs that had long served as medicines among her people. She stood by as her teachers diagnosed and treated the ailments of those who appealed to them for help. And she listened intently as her mother and uncle instructed her in the strict code to which she would have to conform as an eagle doctor. She was never to boast of her skills or offer them to a patient; she must wait instead for

Celebrated Lakota Sioux quilt maker Laura Takes the Gun and her grandson display one of her superb creations, entitled "Flying Sparrow," in front of her home on North Dakota's Standing Rock Reservation. The starburst quilt at right, another of Laura's masterpieces, shows the brilliant use she and other Indian women made of the bright calico fabrics introduced by whites.

those in need to approach her. Furthermore, she was forbidden to demand any fee for her services. Patients seeking the help of an eagle doctor were expected to bring with them ritual offerings of tobacco and green cloth, but any payment beyond that was voluntary and had to be shared by the doctor with others in need. "Don't you ever ask for anything," Sanapia's mother instructed her. "It's going to be given to you."

Sanapia's training concluded when she was 17 with a ceremony that conferred on her special healing powers. During the ritual, her mother placed in her hands live coals, which gave Sanapia the sensation not of searing pain but of an exhilarating chill, working its way up into her arms and carrying with it the gift of healing. Then her mother transmitted power to her mouth by brushing two eagle feathers across her open lips. Thenceforth, Sanapia would carry in her mouth the curative spirit of the creature she called the Medicine Eagle. At the close of the initiation ceremony, Sanapia embarked on a vision quest, leaving home for four days and nights to perform a spiritual vigil on a nearby hillside. In this instance, the quest was a test of courage, for at night in the open, her elders coun-

Mohawk poet Pauline Johnson poses in the fringed buckskin jacket and bear-claw necklace she wore when giving her first dramatic readings in the 1890s. Before her death at age 51 in 1913, she became one of Canada's most beloved orators, touring the country coast to coast and making three successful trips to London.

seled her, she would be prey to ghosts that would wrestle with her and try to steal her medicine. As it turned out, fear got the better of her, and she left the hillside at dusk each evening and spent the night curled up under the front porch of her house.

Sanapia subsequently attributed the difficulties she experienced as a young woman to her failure to confront the ghosts and overcome them. Her first marriage ended in separation, and after her beloved second husband died when she was in her late thirties, she lived at loose ends for a number of years before settling down to a lasting marriage and rededicating herself to healing at about the age of 50. That gift had remained with her throughout her life, but she needed great maturity to apply it. Indeed, the Comanche believed that only after a woman ceased to menstruate could she properly exert the powers conferred on an eagle doctor.

Revered Comanche medicine woman Sanapia, shown here in the 1960s, carried a medicine kit that included not only practical nostrums such as sneezeweed for nasal congestion but also potent charms such as a golden eagle's tail feather, used ritually to cure deeper spiritual and physical ailments.

As a healer, Sanapia was sometimes called upon to treat comparatively simple complaints, to which she applied her extensive knowledge of herbal medicines. Among other remedies, she soothed spider bites by chewing sage leaves and rubbing the wet pulp over the swollen area; numbed the pain of toothaches and burns with a powder derived from prickly ash roots; and eased arthritis, heart pains, and various internal disorders with small doses of peyote, sometimes administered in the form of an infusion, or tea, for the patient to sip.

But her supreme challenge as an eagle doctor was to heal people who were sick in spirit as well as in body—in particular, those who had fallen victim to the paralyzing condition that the Comanche called ghost sickness. That mysterious ailment, which left the victim with a painfully contorted face and sometimes crippled the hands and arms as well, was believed to be caused by restless spirits of the dead that assailed people at night in lonely places. One victim told of being pursued in the dark by a ghost that struck his face and knocked him unconscious; when he came to, his face was numb and twisted.

Sanapia was at times ambivalent about ghosts, but she also understood that ghost sickness was a disorder of the mind and the heart as well as of the flesh. The only way to prevent the sickness, she insisted, was to face the pursuing ghost and defy it. "You got to stand up to that ghost," she emphasized. "You got to show it you ain't afraid of it. If you don't, they got you, and they twist you up." For those who lacked such resolve and fell prey to evil spirits, she offered treatment that was intended both to ease their physical suffering and to restore their composure and courage. Anthropologist David Jones, who studied Sanapia's life and observed her healing techniques, noted that many of those who came to her to be cured of ghost sickness were young men from traditional backgrounds who were torn between ancestral values and the attractions of the outside world. For them, he concluded, coming to Sanapia for help was a way of returning to the tribal fold and seeking absolution there.

A victim of ghost sickness would first appeal to Sanapia through an intermediary, typically an older woman who would state the patient's case and assure Sanapia that her efforts would not go unrewarded. Then the patient would visit, dressed simply and humbly as a gesture of supplication. The patient brought her the traditional gifts of tobacco and green cloth, which served as a symbolic offering to the medicinal plants that she used. Then Sanapia smoked some of the tobacco to signal her acceptance of the patient and said reassuringly, "Tell me your troubles." Burdened with fear and anguish, the patient sometimes spoke of his troubles for hours, while Sanapia offered only expressions of sympathy and refrained from any words or gestures that might convey disapproval, even when her visitor confided thoughts and feelings that struck her as dreadful.

Sanapia then invited the patient to bathe in a nearby stream, change his clothes, and spend the night in her home as a guest of her family. The next morning, she and the patient rose before dawn and walked to a secluded place near her house, where she offered prayers to the earth and the rising sun. "Mother earth, I want you to take my words," she implored.

Crow women wearing special robes decorated with strips of ribbon and rows of buttons or beads attend a meeting of the Tobacco Society, one of the tribe's most prestigious institutions.

Neatly captioned by its Indian artist, a 19th-century drawing shows Crow women marching toward a secret garden plot, some wearing Tobacco Society cloaks, others carrying bundles of sacred tobacco to be planted.

"I want you to do what I want. I'm walking over you. I live on you, and I love you because you're my land." When the sun rose, she addressed it as the "big eagle" and asked it too for help in the task ahead. Then she led her patient back indoors, where she cleansed herself with cedar smoke and took up a Bible, which she had studied in mission school and whose lessons had become part of her faith without supplanting her traditional beliefs. With scripture in hand, she prayed to "God and Jesus and especially the Holy Ghost." Finally, she invoked the aid of the peyote and her other medicines and began to tremble as the healing power came over her.

When the trembling ceased, Sanapia commenced her treatment. She chewed milkweed root and covered the afflicted parts of the patient's body with the juice. Then she chewed milkweed and sage together and applied her mouth to the patient's twisted face in order to suck the sickness out. If the patient's hands were affected as well, she would hold them gently over cedar smoke and sing to him. Such treatments were repeated at midday and at dusk, and frequently they were enough in themselves to bring about a cure. But if the patient showed no signs of improving, she sometimes resorted to stronger measures such as a peyote ritual, during which the patient consumed small amounts of that drug, which was also applied to the afflicted areas in the form of a decoction.

As a last resort, Sanapia appealed to her spiritual patron, the Medicine Eagle. She did so only in stubborn cases, because the eagle's power was thought to be so great that it could cause harm to the patient and to Sanapia herself. If nothing else promised a cure, however, she would seclude herself and meditate on the lessons her mother and uncle had taught her. Come nightfall, she would sit alone in the dark, singing a song she had learned during her apprenticeship. As she sang, she felt the spirits of her mother and uncle approach, and she asked them to intercede for her with the Medicine Eagle. When the eagle drew near, she felt a cold rushing wind, and glimpsed its great feathers, and heard a voice encouraging her to have faith and persist with the cure. Afterward, she returned to the patient and wafted smoke over him with a feather. She did not touch him, for fear of harming him with the power that had entered her. But if the patient recovered, she went outside with him at dawn to greet the sun and offer him a final blessing.

Sanapia could not cure everyone who came to her, and she recognized the limits of her powers. Although ghost sickness resembled the kind of paralysis caused by stroke, she knew the difference and did not attempt to treat victims of stroke, which she defined as a white man's disease and relegated to white doctors. Other patients who visited were beyond the help of any doctor. In such cases, she could hear an inner voice pronouncing the patient's fate: "He's dead right now, he's dead right now." Sanapia seldom shared what she knew with such doomed patients, and in some cases they felt good enough after consulting her to move about and have a meal. "Well, they eat their food and drink water and they feel good," she observed. "But I know that's the last meal they going to have. That's the last drink they going to have."

Between the time she started healing in earnest and her death in 1968, Sanapia treated scores of people for ghost sickness and hundreds for other ailments. But her importance to the community went well beyond the numbers she cured or comforted. For many Comanches, she was proof that the powers claimed by their ancestors were real and enduring. And by confronting the ghosts of the sick, she set an example of courage and conviction for all those haunted by ills of the flesh or spirit to follow.

For Sanapia, honoring ancestral ways was largely a matter of heeding the lessons of her mother and uncle. But other Native American women went beyond what they learned from their elders to reinterpret cultural practices that had lost some of their power in recent times, as whites and their

This unidentified Arikara woman, photographed in 1908, served her tribe as Keeper of the Medicine Bundle. Filled with sacred objects that conferred power on their owners, medicine bundles were acquired by individuals as well as by tribal groups, which appointed honored members to guard the contents.

ways altered tribal societies. Among those who reinvigorated Indian artistic traditions in the 20th century was potter Maria Martinez of New Mexico's San Ildefonso Pueblo. The craft that she excelled at had deep roots among the Pueblo Indians of the Southwest and their cultural predecessors, the cliff-dwelling Anasazi. Women of the region had been molding clay vessels for more than 1,000 years. By the time the San Ildefonso Pueblo emerged along the upper Rio Grande, about the year 1300, potters in the area were turning out vessels of great beauty, which they painted with haunting designs that evoked the life-giving powers of nature—birds and beasts, mountains and clouds, rain and lightning.

This rich cultural tradition was threatened by the arrival in the region of Spaniards and later Anglo-Americans—who brought with them metal cookware and commercially manufactured ceramics and changed the Pueblo economy. By the late 19th century, the number of women who were expert at the craft had dwindled, and most of the pots that were still being produced offered little for the eye to admire. The process of decline was not limited to pottery. Recent developments were endangering much of what the Pueblo peoples had managed to preserve of their heritage since coming in contact with whites.

By accommodating the early Spanish colonizers when necessary—and resisting them when pressed—Pueblo Indians had retained a measure of autonomy that American authorities acknowledged when they took control of the region in the mid-19th century. Federal officials saw no need to uproot the settled villagers from their remote desert homes and move them onto reservations. In 1876 a U.S. Supreme Court ruling deemed the Pueblos "competent Indians" and granted them permission to sell land without interference from the government. The residents of San Ildefonso—and other pueblos—continued to live in adobe houses, built around a central plaza, and to raise corn and other crops in the nearby fields. While most of them faithfully attended the pueblo's Catholic church, they also

Pottery makers Julian and Maria Martinez display their finished wares at their workshop in New Mexico's San Ildefonso Pueblo. In the 1920s and 1930s, the couple perfected the technique of combining a matte black design with a polished black surface, as displayed in the vessel below.

worshiped in underground kivas, just as their ancestors had, beseeching the spirits of nature to bring them good fortune.

The culture that the Pueblo Indians had salvaged was increasingly at risk, however. In the late 1800s, more and more outsiders ignored their property rights and squatted on their land, diminishing harvests that were already impaired by drought. At San Ildefonso, as elsewhere, few families were able to glean enough from the fields to support themselves, and many young men left to seek jobs in the cities, on the railroads, or on ranches. San Ildefonso, which had boasted a population of perhaps 800 in the 17th century, now had barely 100 residents, and those who remained had cause to fear for the future of their community.

Such were the prospects that faced young Maria as she entered adulthood. Born in 1886, she learned about the proud Pueblo ceramic tradition from her great-grandmother—who kept a collection of lovely old pots made at San Ildefonso and nearby communities and bequeathed them to her great-granddaughters—and from her aunt, Tia Nicolasa, a gifted potter who shared her knowledge of the craft with young Maria. In conversations with ethnographer Alice Marriott, who wrote the story of her life, Martinez later recollected how as girls, she and her sister first tried to make dishes for their playhouse from moist clay. The dishes kept cracking when they dried in the sun, so the girls went for help to Tia Nicolasa, who told them that they had to mix sand with the clay.

Tia Nicolasa imparted to the youngsters much else that Pueblo women had learned of the craft of pottery over the centuries—to work in the shade so the clay mixture would stay moist; to start with a flat base, or "tortilla," and then to stack up slender coils of clay to form the wall of the vessel; and to coat the pot with a wet slip of clay to create a smooth surface. In addition, she showed the girls how to fire their earthenware vessels in a pit that was lined with cedarwood and covered with dried cow manure. Before lighting the wood, Nicolasa scattered a handful of cornmeal over the kiln and offered a blessing to the spirits, asking that her pots emerge from the fire well shaped and strong. In years to come, her niece would perpetuate this ritual, scattering cornmeal and uttering a prayer each time she fired her own kiln.

If much of Maria Martinez's artistic inspiration came from home in the person of her aunt, she profited as well by her education and by the contacts it afforded her with the outside world. She first attended government school at the pueblo, where she and her Tewa-speaking classmates learned English, and later went off to a boarding school in Santa Fe to complete her education. Although the city was little more than 20 miles from San Ildefonso, it was a full day's journey in a wagon. For two years, Maria returned home only for vacations. Living away from home simply deepened her attachment to the pueblo, but her education and her sojourn in Santa Fe prepared her to deal with outsiders who had much to offer—including archaeologists and other scholars who were making exciting discoveries about the cultural heritage of her people.

She was fortunate as well to enter into a relationship with a young man from San Ildefonso, Julian Martinez, who shared her artistic temperament. The two were married in 1904 and embarked on a fruitful partnership that expanded on the Pueblo tradition of parity between husbands and wives in their respective spheres. At San Ildefonso, homes belonged to the women and passed from mothers to daughters. The women were responsible for maintaining the household, including replastering the adobe walls, preparing meals, and crafting those household articles that were not obtained from outside the community. Men, for their part, presided over the fields as well as over most civic and ceremonial activities, particularly those that were related to the kivas.

In at least one respect, Julian Martinez departed from the ancestral pattern—he had little interest in farming, which offered diminishing rewards even to those men who were still dedicated to it. He had other gifts, however, that were rooted in the culture of the pueblo, where men had long crafted tools and ceremonial objects and inscribed sacred wall paintings. With encouragement from Maria, who had little flair for decoration, Julian began to paint the pots she molded, demonstrating an artistry that complemented her own. Other talented couples at San Ildefonso collaborated in the same manner— among them potter Martina Montoya and her painter-husband, Florentino, and Tonita Martinez Roybal and her husband, Juan Cruz.

The career of Maria and Julian Martinez received impetus from an archaeological dig they joined in 1908 on the nearby Pajarito Plateau, where an Anasazi village had been discovered. Julian sketched for the archaeologists many of the designs painted on the walls of the cliff dwellings. Maria was asked to

A delicate feather motif rims a luminous vessel made by Maria Martinez's son Adam and his wife, Santana, whom Maria taught to make pottery.

A clay sculpture in the shape of a Zuni bear fetish, with eyes of turquoise, was made by Kathy Sanchez, a member of the fourth generation of the Martinez family to become pottery makers.

make a pot of the same composition as a fragment uncovered at the site. She marveled at the shard: It was so thin and dense it looked as if it had been molded of pure clay. Upon closer inspection, however, she could see that extremely fine sand had been mixed in to temper the clay and keep it from cracking. With help from Tia Nicolasa, she located sand of that quality not far from the pueblo. The grains were so small that they leaked through the sack she brought the sand home in. After sifting dry clay to render it even finer than the sand, she moistened the mixture and kneaded it. She molded it thin, like the ancient fragment, and it held its shape. The pot that emerged was lighter than any she had created before. Julian painted it, using designs and materials much like those employed by the Anasazi—a brush of yucca fibers that he chewed to the desired consistency and a gray paint derived by boiling down the guaco plant. "I like this sort of work," he said to Maria when he was done. "Everything goes with you. Not like plowing, when everything can go against you."

The pots the Martinezes produced in this manner not only pleased the archaeologists but also attracted outside buyers, who were eager to obtain vessels that evoked the splendid creations of the past. But Maria and Julian did not content themselves with simply reconstructing the old style—they evolved their own. Among the pots they created in the classic manner were a few that emerged from the kiln pure black. Pots blackened by the firing process had once been produced at the Santa Clara Pueblo, but the Martinezes did not know how it had been done, and they could only guess as to what accident had caused this phenomenon. After a great deal of experimentation, Julian managed to reproduce the process by using dried manure to damp down the kiln fire without extinguishing it, producing a dense yellow smoke that baked onto the pot's surface and covered it with an indelible black gloss. He subsequently devised a way of decorating the shiny black surface of the pot by painting on designs with a slip before firing; the design emerged as matte black against the lustrous backdrop. This style, known as black-on-black, was popularized by the Martinezes and adopted by other Pueblo potters and painters. Collectors coveted their creations as works of art that paid tribute to the past yet represented something new and elegant.

By the 1930s, pottery was the mainstay of the San Ildefonso Pueblo. Maria Martinez encouraged her neighbors and kin at San Ildefonso to join in the profitable craft. She employed family members as assistants, shared knowledge of the black-on-black technique with those who inquired, and sometimes etched her name on the bottom of pots made by others to ensure that their work brought as high a price as her own. Before long, the women of San Ildefonso were producing large quantities of black-on-black ware, much of it painted by their husbands. Martinez sold their work, along with her own, from a shop adjacent to her house. A government survey in 1936 revealed that half of the employed adults in the pueblo were working as potters and painters or as other artists; two-thirds of the village's income came from arts and crafts.

Julian Martinez died in the winter of 1943. Maria Martinez continued to practice her craft, collaborating with other painters drawn from the ranks of her talented family—first with a daughter-in-law and then, for many years, with her youngest son, who went by his Tewa name, Popovi Da. In 1967 the pottery of San Ildefonso Pueblo was showcased in an exhibition of Indian art in Washington, D.C. The show was called Powhoge, the Tewa name for San Ildefonso—one of the first times the word was used outside the pueblo. Until her death in 1980, near the age of 100, Maria Martinez continued to live in her adobe house at San Ildefonso, a small, slim woman with gray hair cut in the Pueblo style, the front short and framing her face, the back long and tied in a knot. She appreciated the recognition that she and others of her family received from the outside world for their work. But her neighbors paid her a deeper tribute when they spoke of her as they did other women who sustained the community and honored its traditions: They called her simply a Mother of the Pueblo.

D uring recent decades, a number of Native American women have distinguished themselves as leaders not only in the cultural realm but in political circles as well. By the 1980s, women headed more than 10 percent of the nation's tribal councils or boards. In California alone, 22 of the state's tribal groups were governed by women. As politicians, Indian women addressed the problems of the modern world, but they also drew inspiration from the past and served as guardians of their peoples' heritage. Like those women who pursued the healing path or the way of beauty, they brought the wisdom of their ancestors to bear on the demands of a new era.

One woman who achieved political prominence by reaffirming her ties to her people and their traditions was Wilma Mankiller, who returned as an adult to the Cherokee country she had left as a child and went on to

Deeply grateful to the women of their tribe who did so much over the years to keep its rich culture alive, the Crow Nation in 1994 paid tribute to a number of elder women with banquets, ceremonies, and gifts. A dozen of those so honored, ranging in age from 70 to more than 100, are shown at right and on the next two pages, wearing the colorful dresses that became traditional garb in the years after the Crow people were confined on reservations.

FRANCES BENDS

EMMA DON'T MIX

ANNIE COSTA

MARIE PRETTY PAINT

PERA NOT AFRAID

DORTHY YELLOWMULE

ROSE DECRANE TURNS PLENTY

WINONA PLENTY HOOPS

AGNES DEERNOSE

JANET ADAMS

MAE HOUSE

MILDRED OLD CROW

become principal chief of the tribe. Mankiller—whose surname derives from an ancient title of honor for Cherokee warriors—was born in Oklahoma in 1945 on land that had been allotted earlier in the century to her grandfather, John Mankiller, as part of a federal effort to break up the reservations of the Cherokee and neighboring tribes and assimilate the Indians into white society. That allotment process was traumatic for many Cherokees, because they cherished the solidarity and autonomy they had preserved on the reservation after being forcibly removed from their ancestral homeland in the Southeast in the 1830s—an exodus known to posterity as the Trail of Tears.

Nonetheless, John Mankiller and other Cherokees made the best of their allotments and bequeathed to their descendants a sense of pride and distinction. Wilma's father married a white woman, but their children grew up in an atmosphere rich in Cherokee lore. Wilma vividly recalled childhood visits with her paternal aunt, Maggie Gourd, who entranced her with stories of the Yunwi Tsunsdi, or Little People, who lived in the woods and would run off with young children if they felt that the children had been abandoned. Thereafter, Wilma kept a close eye on her younger brothers and sisters whenever they were entrusted to her.

Wilma was separated from her Cherokee friends and relatives in Oklahoma in 1956 when her father decided to move to San Francisco under the auspices of a federal program designed to relocate Indians to urban

At left, Kiowa women take part in the annual Gourd Dance, a ritual held to renew the tribe's spirit and ensure its prosperity. Above, members of the women's auxiliary of the Kiowa warrior society wear special robes to honor veterans of the armed forces.

areas, where they would presumably find economic opportunity and become part of the mainstream culture. Wilma and her siblings were distraught when the time came to leave home. As she put it later, the long, lonesome journey by train to California was their own Trail of Tears. Arriving in San Francisco, they discovered that the Bureau of Indian Affairs had yet to find them an apartment, and they lived temporarily in a run-down hotel. Outside, prostitutes haunted the street corners, homeless people slumped in the doorways, and police and fire sirens howled through the night like wolves. A few weeks later, the family moved into a safer neighborhood. While her father and eldest brother toiled in a factory there, Wilma endured humiliation in school, where children laughed at the name Mankiller and teased her for the way she dressed and talked. At night, she would read aloud to her sister, attempting to eliminate from her speech any trace of her ancestry.

In the difficult years to come, however, she took comfort in memories of her upbringing in Cherokee country and in the realization that there were other Indians around the city who were finding the adjustment to urban life as painful as she and her siblings were. Many of them began to question whether their assimilation into the larger society was possible, or even desirable. Contrary to the intentions of the relocation program, the Indians became increasingly conscious of their separate status and skeptical of the promises of white authorities. As a teenager, Wilma Mankiller found company at San Francisco's American Indian Center, where she communed with others who felt uprooted and alienated by the relocation effort. Then as she entered adulthood, her discontent crystallized into commitment when Indians of various tribal backgrounds occupied Alcatraz Island in the fall of 1969. The protest, which signaled the growing determination of Native Americans to reclaim their cultural heritage and assert their political rights, inspired Mankiller to become part of that movement. For several years, she ran the Native American Youth

First woman chief of the Cherokee people, Wilma Mankiller worked tirelessly to improve the lot of her people and to plead their cause in many appearances before the United States Congress. She drew inspiration from such powerful Cherokee women of the past as the beloved Nancy Ward.

Center in Oakland and organized a legal defense for Indians living along California's Pit River, who were challenging the right of a utility company to use their ancestral land for a hydroelectric project.

Although her work in California brought Mankiller in touch with members of diverse tribes and left her with a lasting appreciation for their common interests, she found herself longing to return to Cherokee country. The troubled marriage she had entered into in her late teens—with an immigrant from Ecuador who had little sympathy for her career as an activist—ended in divorce in 1974, and two years later, she moved with her two daughters to her native state. She knew that she had regained her old pride of place when she walked past the county courthouse in Stilwell, Oklahoma, and heard an old Cherokee there say to his companions, "There goes John Mankiller's granddaughter."

In the years ahead, Wilma Mankiller did much to honor the spirit of her Cherokee ancestors. After the Trail of Tears, the Cherokee had bravely reconstructed their society, establishing prosperous farms and businesses and erecting schools. In the early 1980s, Mankiller helped organize a project that gave the residents of a poor Cherokee community a chance to do something similar by building and rehabilitating homes and laying 16 miles of pipeline that provided many families there with running water for the first time. The project not only brought Mankiller recognition within the tribe but also introduced her to her future husband, Charlie Soap, a fellow Cherokee organizer who respected her leadership role.

In 1985 she became the first woman to serve as principal chief of the Cherokee, when the acting chief, Ross Swimmer, resigned to take charge of the Bureau of Indian Affairs. She twice won reelection to her leadership position, most recently in 1991, when she received the endorsement of nearly 83 percent of the Cherokee voters. By that time, the Cherokee government had assumed responsibility from the Bureau of Indian Affairs for administering federal funds to the Cherokee people. At her inaugural in 1991, Mankiller could speak realistically of something that had seemed beyond reach when she was growing up—a resurgent Cherokee Nation that lived up to the hopes and sacrifices of generations past. ◆

Sandstone pinna-
cles overlook the
piñon-covered hills
where the Ramah
Navajo women
graze their sheep.
Two co-op members
(above) display their
creation—a weaving
that depicts cere-
monial dancers.

WEAVING OLD WAYS WITH NEW

In November 1984, 17 women from the Ramah Navajo Reservation in west-central New Mexico founded the Ramah Navajo Weavers Association in an effort to bring greater self-reliance and economic independence to their people. Today the cooperative includes more than 40 members spanning five generations. Viewing their craft as a total way of life, the women combine Navajo traditions with new technologies and business practices. While using time-honored methods of sheep raising, wool preparation, and weaving, the women also experiment with modern agricultural techniques. They have established a successful breeding program to improve the quality of their flocks, and they are also developing various range management and land improvement systems to rebuild the soil and maintain healthy grazing lands. Before the creation of the cooperative, the women sold their work through non-Indian middlemen and often received as little as one-fifth of the final price. Now they market their weavings collectively.

Many of their creations—which may be rectangular or square, and range in size from miniatures of five by six inches to rug-size pieces up to eight feet long—are made with wool from the Navajo churro sheep, a rare breed considered the ancestral sheep of the Navajo people. The long, coarse fibers of the churro's double coat of wool are ideally suited for hand carding and hand spinning, and come naturally in several earth tones as well as ebony black. And since the churro wool contains less lanolin than that of other breeds, it is easier to dye by hand.

At the heart of the cooperative's activities is the fundamental notion that Mother Earth is sacred and the source of all life. The Ramah Reservation women carry out their annual cycle of work with blessings, prayers, and utmost respect, thus ensuring that future generations, as well as the present, will be provided for. "We weave—expressing the beauty and order of life," a cooperative statement reads. "We pray, we sing for our own survival and for the survival of this land and people."

A great-grandmother named Katie Henio (left) leads her flock of 150 animals—sheep and a few goats—to pasture. Accompanied by several dogs to assist in herding, Katie rides the land in all kinds of weather and cooks her meals over an open fire. She carries a .22-caliber rifle to ward off coyotes.

Susie Garcia bottle-feeds her hungry lambs. Orphaned lambs are bottle-fed three times a day for the first four months of their lives, then they fend for themselves.

Annie Pino tosses feed to her flock in the corral near her home. Later in the day, she will take them into the countryside to graze.

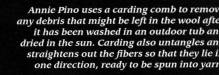

Annie Pino uses a carding comb to remov
any debris that might be left in the wool afte
it has been washed in an outdoor tub an
dried in the sun. Carding also untangles an
straightens out the fibers so that they lie i
one direction, ready to be spun into yarn

*In the shed behind the family corral, young-
sters watch and learn as Katie Henio shears
one of her sheep with handblades. Having
clipped its thick belly wool, she removes the
rest of the fleece in a single piece, all the
while calming the animal with soft words.*

*Annie Pino spins carded wool into yarn b
stretching and twisting it with one han
while rolling the spindle stick with the othe
Yarn created by this age-old method i
often spun a second time in order to thin i
Thick yarn is used for saddle blanket
medium for rugs, and thin for tapestrie*

Lorraine Wayne gathers Navajo tea, a long, spiky herb used to color the newly spun wool a rich orange or a golden earth tone. Because wild plants are considered one of the original gifts from the Holy People, Navajos handle them reverently, never picking more than they need.

Tending her dye pots over an outdoor fire, Annie Pino checks the coloring that has been produced by a bundle of Navajo tea. Each batch of dye is unique in color. The herb madder produces peach tones; dried cactus bugs, deep reds and burgundies; ripe cactus fruit, pinks; walnut shells, browns; juniper berries, snakeweed, and wild carrot, yellows; and the indigo plant, blues.

Using wool that she has washed, carded, spun, and dyed by hand, Elsie Martinez weaves on a traditional Navajo loom in her home. Her design originates from an old pattern, whose name in Navajo means "moving back and forth." It requires 20 days to prepare yarn, and 30 to 40 days to complete a medium-size (30 by 60 inches) weaving.

Working outside her log hogan, Lorraine Wayne strings yarn to both ends of her loom before setting it upright to begin her weaving. Called warping, this process provides a vertical framework for the piece. The warp yarns will be interwoven with the weft, or horizontal, threads.

Esther Rafelito thanks a customer for purchasing a co-op weaving at the annual Santa Fe Indian Market, where the Ramah Navajo Weavers Association markets some of its creations. In 1994 two co-op members received awards for their handiwork.

All of the Ramah Navajo weavings, like the samples opposite, reflect the Navajo principles of balance and harmony. The creation at right, entitled "Stripes," was inspired by the traditional Chief Blanket motif, as was the Liberty Blanket shown below, with which the weavers commemorated the centennial of the Statue of Liberty in 1986.

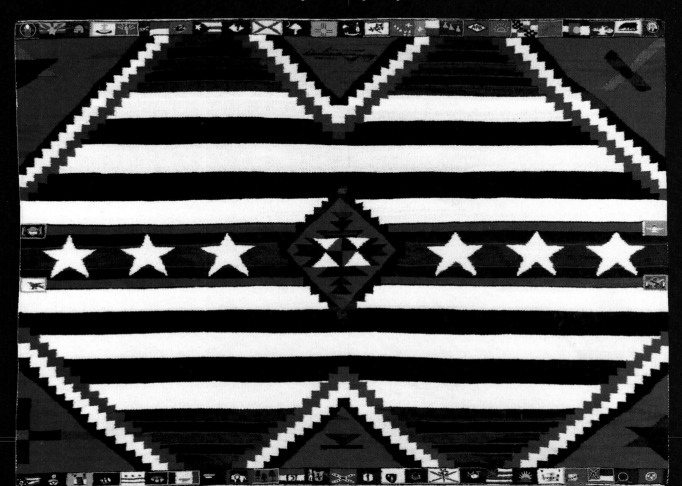

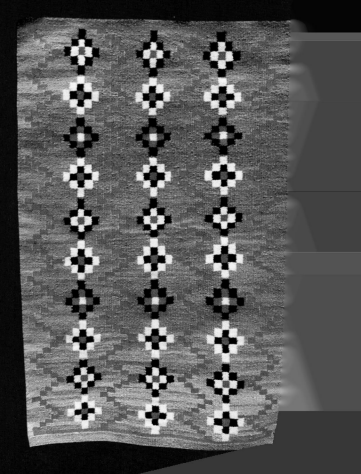

ACKNOWLEDGMENTS

The editors wish to thank the following individuals and institutions for their valuable assistance:

In the United States:
Alaska: Fairbanks—Marge Heath, Elmer E. Ras-muson Library, University of Alaska Fairbanks.
Montana: Billings—C. Adrian Heidenreich, Montana State University. Browning—Daryl Kipp, Piegan Institute.
New Mexico: Pine Hill—Yin-May Lee.
Oklahoma: Tulsa—John R. Wilson. Lawton—Delores Twohatchet.

Washington, D.C.: Vyrtis Thomas, National Anthropological Archives, Smithsonian Institution.
Washington State: Seattle—Rebecca Andrews, Robin K. Wright, The Burke Museum. Tacoma—Elaine Miller, Joy Wernicke, Washington State Historical Society.

BIBLIOGRAPHY

BOOKS
Albers, Patricia, and Beatrice Medicine, *The Hidden Half.* Lanham, Md.: University Press of America, 1983.
Allen, Paula Gunn:
The Sacred Hoop. Boston: Beacon Press, 1992.
Grandmothers of the Light. Boston: Beacon Press, 1991.
Bad Heart Bull, Amos, and Helen H. Blish, *A Pictographic History of the Oglala Sioux.* Lincoln: University of Nebraska Press, 1967.
Bahti, Tom, *Southwestern Indian Ceremonials.* Las Vegas, Nev.: KC Publications, 1982.
Barbour, Philip L., *Pocahontas and Her World.* Boston: Houghton Mifflin, 1970.
Bataille, Gretchen M., ed., *Native American Women.* New York: Garland Publishing, 1993.
Bataille, Gretchen M., and Kathleen M. Sands, *American Indian Women.* New York: Garland Publishing, 1991.
Beck, Peggy V., Anna Lee Walters, and Nia Francisco, *The Sacred.* Tsaile, Ariz.: Navajo Community College Press, 1992.
Boyer, Ruth McDonald, and Narcissus Duffy Gayton, *Apache Mothers and Daughters.* Norman: University of Oklahoma Press, 1992.
Braund, Kathryn E. Holland, *Deerskins & Duffels.* Lincoln: University of Nebraska Press, 1993.
Buchanan, Kimberly Moore, *Apache Women Warriors.* El Paso: Texas Western Press, 1986.
Buckley, Thomas, and Alma Gottlieb, eds., *Blood Magic.* Berkeley: University of California Press, 1988.
Catlin, George:
Episodes from Life among the Indians and Last Rambles. Ed. by Marvin C. Ross. Norman: University of Oklahoma Press, 1959.
Letters and Notes on the Manners, Customs, and Conditions of the North American Indians. Vol. 2. New York: Dover Publications, 1973.
Clifton, James A., ed., *Being and Becoming Indian.* Chicago: Dorsey Press, 1989.
Coleman, Michael C., *American Indian Children at School, 1850-1930.* Jackson: University Press of Mississippi, 1993.
Cox, Bruce Alden, ed., *Native People, Native Lands.* Ottawa, Ont.: Carleton University Press, 1988.
Crary, Margaret, *Susette La Flesche.* New York: Hawthorn Books, 1973.
Cuero, Delfina, *The Autobiography of Delfina Cuero.* Morongo Indian Reservation, Calif.: Malki Museum Press, 1970.
Cycles of Life, by the Editors of Time-Life Books (The American Indians series). Alexandria, Va.: Time-Life Books, 1994.

Dancing Colors. San Francisco: Chronicle Books, 1992.
Denig, Edwin Thompson, *Five Indian Tribes of the Upper Missouri.* Ed. by John C. Ewers. Norman: University of Oklahoma Press, 1961.
Driver, Harold E., *Indians of North America.* Chicago: University of Chicago Press, 1969.
Etienne, Mona, and Eleanor Leacock, eds., *Women and Colonization.* New York: Praeger, 1980.
Felton, Harold W., *Nancy Ward, Cherokee.* New York: Dodd, Mead, 1975.
Fogelson, Raymond D., "On the 'Petticoat Government' of the Eighteenth-Century Cherokee," in *Personality and the Cultural Construction of Society.* Ed. by David K. Jordan and Marc J. Swartz. Tuscaloosa: University of Alabama Press, 1990.
Fogelson, Raymond D., and Richard N. Adams, eds., *The Anthropology of Power.* New York: Academic Press, 1977.
Foreman, Carolyn Thomas, *Indian Women Chiefs.* Washington, D.C.: Zenger Publishing, 1976 (reprint of 1954 edition).
Foster, W. Garland, *The Mohawk Princess.* Vancouver, B.C.: Lions' Gate Publishing, 1931.
Garbarino, Merwyn S., *The Seminole.* New York: Chelsea House Publishers, 1989.
Gilman, Carolyn, and Mary Jane Schneider, *The Way to Independence.* St. Paul: Minnesota Historical Society Press, 1987.
Green, Rayna:
Native American Women. Bloomington: Indiana University Press, 1983.
Women in American Indian Society. New York: Chelsea House Publishers, 1992.
Gridley, Marion E., *American Indian Women.* New York: Hawthorn Books, 1974.
Grinnell, George Bird, *The Cheyenne Indians.* Vol. 2. Lincoln: University of Nebraska Press, 1972 (reprint of 1923 edition).
Guthrie, Patricia, "Weaving the Big One," in *Indians of New Mexico.* Ed. by R. C. Sandoval and Ree Sheck. Santa Fe: New Mexico Magazine, 1990.
Hamilton, Milton W., *Sir William Johnson.* Port Washington, N.Y.: Kennikat Press, 1976.
Hassrick, Royal B., *The Sioux.* Norman: University of Oklahoma Press, 1964.
Highwater, Jamake, *Ritual of the Wind.* Toronto: Methuen Publications, 1984.
Hirschfelder, Arlene, and Paulette Molin, *The Encyclopedia of Native American Religions.* New York: Facts On File, 1992.
Horan, James D., *The McKenney-Hall Portrait Gallery of American Indians.* New York: Bramhall House, 1986.
Howard, James H., *Shawnee!* Athens: Ohio University Press, 1981.
Hoxie, Frederick E., *A Final Promise.* Lincoln: University of Nebraska Press, 1984.
Hudson, Charles, *The Southeastern Indians.* Knoxville: University of Tennessee Press, 1976.
Hultkrantz, Åke, *Native Religions of North America.* San Francisco: Harper, 1987.
Hungry Wolf, Adolf, *The Blood People.* New York: Harper & Row, 1977.
Hungry Wolf, Adolf, and Beverly Hungry Wolf, *Shadows of the Buffalo.* New York: William Morrow, 1983.
Hungry Wolf, Beverly, *The Ways of My Grandmothers.* New York: William Morrow, 1980.
International Congress of Anthropological and Ethnological Sciences, 9th, Chicago, 1973, *Being Female.* Ed. by Dana Raphael. The Hague: Mouton Publishers, 1975.
Iverson, Peter, *The Navajos.* New York: Chelsea House Publishers, 1990.
Jones, Charles, ed., *Look To the Mountain Top.* San Jose, Calif.: Gousha Publications, 1972.
Jones, David E., *Sanapia.* New York: Holt, Rinehart and Winston, 1972.
Josephy, Alvin M. Jr., ed., *The American Heritage Book of Indians.* New York: American Heritage Publishing, 1961.
Keller, Betty, *Pauline.* Vancouver, B.C.: Douglas & McIntyre, 1981.
Kelsay, Isabel Thompson, *Joseph Brant, 1743-1807.* Syracuse, N.Y.: Syracuse University Press, 1984.
Laubin, Reginald, and Gladys Laubin, *The Indian Tipi.* Norman: University of Oklahoma Press, 1977.
Lee, Richard B., and Irven DeVore, eds., *Man the Hunter.* Chicago: Aldine Publishing, 1968.
Linderman, Frank B., *Pretty-Shield.* Lincoln: University of Nebraska Press, 1972 (reprint of 1932 edition).
Lyford, Carrie A., *Quill and Beadwork of the Western Sioux.* Ed. by Willard W. Beatty. Boulder, Colo.: Johnson Books, 1979 (reprint of 1940 edition).
McCracken, Harold, *George Catlin and the Old Frontier.* New York: Dial Press, 1959.
McGaa, Ed, *Mother Earth Spirituality.* San Francisco: Harper, 1990.
McGreevy, Susan Brown, *Maria.* Santa Fe, N.Mex.: Sunstone Press, 1982.
Mankiller, Wilma, and Michael Wallis, *Mankiller.* New York: St. Martin's Press, 1993.
Margolin, Malcolm, ed., *The Way We Lived.* Berkeley: Heyday Books, 1981.
Marriott, Alice, *María.* Norman: University of Oklahoma Press, 1948.
Matthiasson, Carolyn J., ed., *Many Sisters.* New York: Free Press, 1974.
Maurer, Evan M., *Visions of the People.* Minneapolis: The Minneapolis Institute of Arts, 1992.
Meighan, Clement W., and Francis A. Riddell, *The*

Maru Cult of the Pomo Indians. Los Angeles: Southwest Museum, 1972.

Miller, Alfred J., *Braves and Buffalo.* Toronto: University of Toronto Press, 1973.

Miller, Jay, *Shamanic Odyssey.* Menlo Park, Calif.: Ballena Press, 1988.

Miller, Jay, ed., *Mourning Dove.* Lincoln: University of Nebraska Press, 1990.

Modesto, Ruby, and Guy Mount, *Not For Innocent Ears.* Angelus Oaks, Calif.: Sweetlight Books, 1980.

Morgen, Sandra, ed., *Gender and Anthropology.* Washington, D.C.: American Anthropological Association, 1989.

Mossiker, Frances, *Pocahontas.* New York: Alfred A. Knopf, 1976.

Nelson, Mary Carroll, *Maria Martinez.* Minneapolis: Dillon Press, 1972.

Niethammer, Carolyn, *Daughters of the Earth.* New York: Macmillan, 1977.

Ortiz, Alfonso, ed., *Southwest.* Vol. 10 of *Handbook of North American Indians.* Washington, D.C.: Smithsonian Institution, 1983.

Oswalt, Robert L., *Kashaya Texts.* Berkeley: University of California Press, 1964.

Pulford, Florence, *Morning Star Quilts.* Los Altos, Calif.: Leone Publications, 1989.

Reiter, Rayna R., ed., *Toward an Anthropology of Women.* New York: Monthly Review Press, 1975.

Roessel, Ruth, *Women in Navajo Society.* Rough Rock, Ariz.: Navajo Resource Center, 1981.

The Spirit Sings. Toronto: McClelland and Stewart and Glenbow Museum, 1987.

Stepney, Philip H. R., and David J. Goa, eds., *The Scriver Blackfoot Collection.* Edmonton: Provincial Museum of Alberta, 1990.

Stockel, H. Henrietta, *Women of the Apache Nation.* Reno: University of Nevada Press, 1991.

Suttles, Wayne, ed., *Northwest Coast.* Vol. 7 of *Handbook of North American Indians.* Washington, D.C.: Smithsonian Institution, 1990.

Swanton, John R., *The Indians of the Southeastern United States.* Washington, D.C.: Smithsonian Institution Press, 1979.

Sweet, Jill D., *Dances of the Tewa Pueblo Indians.* Santa Fe, N.Mex.: School of American Research Press, 1985.

Taylor, Colin F., ed., *The Native Americans.* New York: Smithmark, 1991.

Thomson, Peggy, *Katie Henio.* New York: Cobblehill Books, 1994.

Todd, Helen, *Mary Musgrove.* Savannah: Seven Oaks, 1981.

Underhill, Ruth M., *Red Man's Religion.* Chicago: University of Chicago Press, 1965.

Van Kirk, Sylvia, *"Many Tender Ties."* Winnipeg, Man.: Watson & Dwyer Publishing, 1980.

Van Steen, Marcus, *Pauline Johnson.* Toronto: Musson, 1965.

Wildschut, William, *Crow Indian Medicine Bundles.* Ed. by John C. Ewers. New York: Museum of the American Indian, 1975.

Wilson, Gilbert L., *Buffalo Bird Woman's Garden.* St. Paul: Minnesota Historical Society Press, 1987.

Wood, Marion, *Spirits, Heroes & Hunters from North American Indian Mythology.* New York: Schocken Books, 1982.

Wood, Peter H., Gregory A. Waselkov, and M. Thomas Hatley, eds., *Powhatan's Mantle.* Lincoln: University of Nebraska Press, 1989.

Woodward, Grace Steele, *Pocahontas.* Norman: University of Oklahoma Press, 1969.

Wright, J. Leitch Jr., *The Only Land They Knew.* New York: Free Press, 1981.

PERIODICALS

Anderson, Karen, "Commodity Exchange and Subordination: Montagnais-Naskapi and Huron Women, 1600-1650." *Signs,* Autumn 1985.

Anderson, Robert, "The Northern Cheyenne War Mothers." *Anthropological Quarterly,* Vol. 29, 1956.

Beauchamp, William, "Iroquois Women." *The Journal of American Folk-lore,* April-June 1900.

Brown, Judith K., "Economic Organization and the Position of Women among the Iroquois." *Ethnohistory,* Summer-Fall 1970.

Buffalohead, Priscilla K., "Farmers, Warriors, Traders: A Fresh Look at Ojibway Women." *Minnesota History,* Summer 1983.

"Cherokee Losing Chief Who Revitalized Tribe." *The New York Times,* April 6, 1994.

Ewers, John C., "Deadlier than the Male." *American Heritage,* June 1965.

Green, Norma Kidd, "Four Sisters: Daughters of Joseph LaFlesche." *Nebraska History,* June 1964.

Green, Rayna, "The Pocahontas Perplex: The Image of Indian Women in American Culture." *The Massachusetts Review,* Autumn 1975.

Grinnell, George Bird, "Cheyenne Woman Customs." *American Anthropologist,* Vol. 4, 1902.

Gundy, H. Pearson, "Molly Brant, Loyalist." *Ontario History,* Summer 1953.

Hamamsy, Laila Shukry, "The Role of Women in a Changing Navaho Society." *American Anthropologist,* Vol. 59, 1957.

Helms, M. W., "Matrilocality, Social Solidarity, and Culture Contact: Three Case Histories." *Southwestern Journal of Anthropology,* Summer 1970.

Johnston, Jean, "Molly Brant: Mohawk Matron." *Ontario History,* June 1964.

Kehoe, Alice B.:

"The Metonymic Pole and Social Roles." *Journal of Anthropological Research,* Winter 1973.

"Old Woman Had Great Power." *The Western Canadian Journal of Anthropology,* Vol. 6, 1976.

Klein, Alan M., "The Plains Truth: The Impact of Colonialism on Indian Women." *Dialectical Anthropology,* February 1983.

Klein, Laura F., " 'She's One of Us, You Know': The Public Life of Tlingit Women: Traditional, Historical, and Contemporary Perspectives." *The Western Canadian Journal of Anthropology,* Vol. 6, 1976.

Leacock, Eleanor, "Women's Status in Egalitarian Society: Implications for Social Evolution." *Current Anthropology,* June 1978.

Lessard, F. Dennis, "Plains Pictographic Art: A Source of Ethnographic Information." *American Indian Art Magazine,* Spring 1992.

Lewis, Oscar, "Manly-Hearted Women among the North Piegan." *American Anthropologist,* Vol. 43, 1941.

McClary, Ben Harris, "Nancy Ward: The Last Beloved Woman of the Cherokees." *Tennessee Historical Quarterly,* December 1962.

Mathes, Valerie Sherer:

"Native American Women in Medicine and the Military." *Journal of the West,* April 1982.

"A New Look at the Role of Women in Indian Society." *American Indian Quarterly,* Vol. 2, 1979.

Michelson, Truman, "The Narrative of a Southern Cheyenne Woman." *Smithsonian Miscellaneous Collections,* March 21, 1932.

Nelson, Ann T., "Woman in Groups: Women's Ritual Sodalities in Native North America." *The Western Canadian Journal of Anthropology,* Vol. 6, 1976.

Nowak, Barbara, "Women's Roles and Status in a Changing Iroquois Society." *Occasional Papers in Anthropology,* April 1979.

Parrish, Otis, and Paula Hammett, "Parrish: A Pomo Shaman." *Native Self-Sufficiency,* September 1981.

Perry, Richard J., "The Fur Trade and the Status of Women in the Western Subarctic." *Ethnohistory,* Fall 1979.

Raczka, Paul M., "Sacred Robes of the Blackfoot and Other Northern Plains Tribes." *American Indian Art Magazine,* Summer 1992.

Schlegel, Alice:

"The Adolescent Socialization of the Hopi Girl." *Ethnology,* October 1973.

"Sexual Antagonism among the Sexually Egalitarian Hopi." *Ethos,* Summer 1979.

Tanner, Helen Hornbeck, "Coocoochee: Mohawk Medicine Woman." *American Indian Culture and Research Journal,* Vol. 3, 1979.

Tucker, Norma, "Nancy Ward, Ghighau of the Cherokees." *The Georgia Historical Quarterly,* June 1969.

Voegelin, C. F., "The Shawnee Female Deity." *Yale University Publications in Anthropology,* 1936.

Voegelin, C. F., and E. W. Voegelin, "The Shawnee Female Deity in Historical Perspective." *American Anthropologist,* July-September 1944.

Wissler, Clark, "Societies and Dance Associations of the Blackfoot Indians." *Anthropological Papers of the American Museum of Natural History,* Vol. 11, 1913.

OTHER PUBLICATIONS

Albers, Patricia, and Jeanne Kay, "Gender and Systems of Property Ownership among Indians of the Upper Middle West." Unpublished manuscript. 1991.

Basso, Keith H., "The Gift of Changing Woman." *Smithsonian Institution Bureau of American Ethnology Bulletin 196.* Washington, D.C.: United States Government Printing Office, 1966.

Randle, Martha Champion, "Iroquois Women, Then and Now." *Smithsonian Institution Bureau of American Ethnology Bulletin 149.* Washington, D.C.: United States Government Printing Office, 1951.

Richards, Cara B., "Matriarchy or Mistake: The Role of Iroquois Women through Time." *Cultural Stability and Cultural Change.* Proceedings of the 1957 Annual Spring Meeting of the American Ethnological Society. Seattle: University of Washington Press, 1957.

Straus, Anne Sawyier, "Being Human in the Cheyenne Way." Doctoral dissertation. Chicago: University of Chicago, March 1976.

Sullivan, Dorothy Tidwell, "Cherokee Heritage Collection." Norman, Oklahoma: Memory Circle Studio.

PICTURE CREDITS

The sources for the illustrations that appear in this book are listed below. Credits from left to right are separated by semicolons; from top to bottom they are separated by dashes.

Cover: Steve Hanks. **6:** National Anthropological Archives (NAA), Smithsonian Institution, neg. no. 2987-A-3. **7:** San Diego Museum of Man, neg. no. 16059. **8:** Library of Congress. **9:** Southwest Museum, Los Angeles, photo no. N.22991. **10:** The Charles Bunnell Collection, acc. no. 58-1026-2403, Archives, Alaska and Polar Regions Department, University of Alaska Fairbanks. **11:** NAA, Smithsonian Institution, neg. no. 76-6644. **12, 13:** NAA, Smithsonian Institution, neg. nos. 54928; 56118. **14, 15:** NAA, Smithsonian Institution, neg. nos. T-15373; 76-15821. **16:** Phoebe Apperson Hearst Museum of Anthropology, University of California at Berkeley, neg. no. 3039. **17:** Library of Congress. **18:** Fred Hirschmann—reproduced from *A Pictographic History of the Oglala Sioux* by Amos Bad Heart Bull, text by Helen H. Blish, by permission of the University of Nebraska Press. © 1967 by the University of Nebraska Press. **20:** The Bettmann Archive. **22:** NAA, Smithsonian Institution, neg. no. 996-D-1; Nina Berman/SIPA Press. **23:** Larry Sherer, courtesy Buffalo Gallery, Inc. **24:** Delores Twohatchet—The Henry Huntington Library and Art Gallery. **25:** NAA, Smithsonian Institution, neg. no. 56388. **27:** Denver Public Library, Western History Department. **28, 29:** Courtesy Thomas Burke Memorial Washington State Museum, catalog nos. BWSM 1-1583; BWSM 1993-85/2. **30:** NAA, Smithsonian Institution, neg. no. 448. **31:** Missouri Historical Society, St. Louis, Kiowa Camp Life. Acc. no. 1880.13.41. **34, 35:** NAA, Smithsonian Institution, neg. nos. 73-9775; 41106. **37:** NAA, Smithsonian Institution, neg. no. 55498. **38, 39:** Dorothy Sullivan. **40:** NAA, Smithsonian Institution, neg. no. 56830. **41:** John Eastcott/Yva Momatiuk. **42, 43:** Charles H. Barstow Collection, Eastern Montana College, photographed by Michael Crummett. **44:** Alexis Duclos/Gamma Liaison. **45:** National Museum of American Art/Art Resource, New York. **46:** NAA, Smithsonian Institution, neg. no. 3084. **47:** The Montreal Museum of Fine Arts, neg. no. 1947.991. **48:** Library of Congress, USZ-62-64853. **49:** Norman Bancroft-Hunt. **50:** Photo by Ben Wittick, School of American Research Collections in the Museum of New Mexico, neg. no. 15959. **51:** The National Museum of Denmark, Department of Ethnography. Photographer: Kit Weiss (2). **53:** NAA, Smithsonian Institution, neg. no. 76-15880. **55:** Delores Twohatchet. **57:** Lee Marmon. **58:** Dennis L. Sanders. **59:** © Monty Roessel. **60, 61:** Murv Jacob. **62, 63:** NAA, Smithsonian Institution, neg. no. 57231-A; photo by Millie Knapp, courtesy *Turtle Quarterly* (2); Richard Erdoes. **64, 65:** Nebraska State Historical Society; Richard Erdoes—© Michael Crummett. **66, 67:** National Museum of the American Indian, Smithsonian Institution, no. 2/6928; Ruthe Blalock Jones—Kansas City Museum, Kansas City, Missouri, Bruce Bandle, photographer. **68:** School of American Research, Santa Fe, New Mexico, catalog no. IAF.P.91. **69:** Branson Reynolds, Durango, Colorado—Roger Sweet; John R. Wilson Collection. **70:** Wheelwright Museum of the American Indian—private collection, photo courtesy Native American Painting Reference Library. **71:** © Monty Roessel (2). **72:** Photo by Ben Wittick, School of American Research Collections in the Museum of New Mexico, neg. no. 16212—Southwest Museum, Los Angeles, photo no. N.24883—J. R. Willis, courtesy Museum of New Mexico, neg. no. 42111. **73:** Edward S. Curtis, courtesy Museum of New Mexico, neg. no. 31961. **74, 75:** NAA, Smithsonian Institution, neg. no. 54589; UPI/Bettmann—NAA, Smithsonian Institution, neg. nos. 53506-C; 45331. **76, 77:** Courtesy Museum of New Mexico, neg. no. 44178; H. Armstrong Roberts, Inc. (2)—Southwest Museum, Los Angeles, photo no. N.24363. **78, 79:** Neg. no. 19853 (photo by A. Skinner), courtesy Department of Library Services, American Museum of Natural History; courtesy Patricia Albers—Minnesota Historical Society, neg. nos. 35773; 1902. **80, 81:** Montana Historical Society, Helena, neg. no. 955-523; The Granger Collection, New York—neg. no. 127921, courtesy Department of Library Services, American Museum of Natural History—NAA, Smithsonian Institution, neg. no. 42022. **82:** Photo by Ben Wittick, School of American Research Collections in the Museum of New Mexico, neg. no. 16331. **85:** Eiteljorg Museum of American Indian and Western Art, Indianapolis, Indiana. **86:** San Diego Museum of Man, neg. no. 24893. **88:** The Granger Collection, New York. **89:** National Museum of American Art/Art Resource, New York—George Catlin/courtesy Art Resource/National Musem of American Art/gift from Mrs. Joseph Harrison Jr. **90, 91:** NAA, Smithsonian Institution, neg. no. 75-14716. **93:** Neg. no. 286500, courtesy Department of Library Services, American Museum of Natural History, New York. **94, 95:** Joslyn Art Museum, Omaha, Nebraska, gift of the Enron Art Foundation (2). **97:** Canada Post. **98:** National Museum of American Art, Washington, D.C./Art Resource, New York. **99:** San Diego Museum of Man. **101:** Courtesy Little Bighorn Battlefield National Monument; John C. Ewers—Paul S. Conklin. **102:** Montana Historical Society, Helena, neg. no. 941-819. **104, 105:** Bob Scriver; photograph courtesy National Museum of the American Indian, Smithsonian Institution, photo no. 36878—neg. no. 319795, courtesy Department of Library Services, American Museum of Natural History. **106:** Library of Congress, USZ-62-101191—Library of Congress, American Museum of Natural History, Anthropological Papers, Vol. II, part 4, p. 431 and p. 433. **107:** Library of Congress, American Museum of Natural History, Anthropological Papers, Vol. II, part 4, p. 431 and p. 432.—neg. no. 122883 (photo by A. J. Rota), courtesy Department of Library Services, American Museum of Natural History, New York—neg. no. 122754, courtesy Department of Library Services, American Museum of Natural History, New York. **108, 109:** Photo by Ben Wittick, School of American Research Collections in the Museum of New Mexico, neg. no. 15955; San Diego Museum of Man, no. 24906. **110:** Frank Fieber, North Light—Canadian Museum of Civilization, neg. no. J-4386. **111:** NAA, Smithsonian Institution, neg. no. 43,161. **112:** John Rice Irwin, Museum of Appalachia. **114,** **115:** Library of Congress; photos by Jerome J. Simone, Executive Director, United Indian Health Service, arrangements by Darlene Magee, Yurok Tribe (5)—photo by A. W. Ericson, courtesy the Peter E. Palmquist Collection. **116:** NAA, Smithsonian Institution, neg. no. 76-4665—neg. no. 242717, courtesy Department of Library Services, American Museum of Natural History, New York—Shannon Gray; Mark O. Rosacker, Wild Life Culturist. **117:** Adolph Greenberg. **118:** Neg. no. 317351 (photo by Joseph K. Dixon), courtesy Department of Library Services, American Museum of Natural History, New York—Latonna Big Lake; Robin D. Vallie. **119:** Dennis L. Sanders. **120, 121:** Library of Congress, USZ-62-99793; Washington State Historical Society, Tacoma—Joe Cantrell, Portland, Oregon (3). **122, 123:** Library of Congress; Michael Chiago/The Heard Museum and Archives—P. K. Weis (4). **124, 125:** Arizona State Museum, University of Arizona—Roger Sweet. **127:** Phoebe Apperson Hearst Museum of Anthropology, University of California at Berkeley, neg. no. 15-25500. **128:** Ruby Modesto and Guy Mount—NAA, Smithsonian Institution, neg. no. 996-D-4—John Running. **129:** NAA, Smithsonian Institution, neg. no. 395-A—NAA, Smithsonian Institution, neg. no. 76-16272. **130, 131:** John Eastcott/Yva Momatiuk—courtesy Thomas Burke Memorial Washington State Museum, catalog no. BWSM 2425; Bob Scriver, photo by Marshall Noice—Michael Crummett, courtesy Chief Plenty Coups State Park Museum, Pryor, Montana (2). **132, 133:** Jana Harcharek, Barrow, Alaska; Paul S. Conklin (2); © Monty Roessel—Paul B. Steinmetz, S.J. **135:** Peabody Museum, Harvard University; Phoebe Apperson Hearst Museum of Anthropology, University of California at Berkeley, neg. no. 23209. **136, 137:** National Museum of the American Indian, Smithsonian Institution, neg. no. 2499—Roger Sweet. **139:** NAA, Smithsonian Institution, neg. no. 764329. **140, 141:** Richard Erdoes; courtesy the Glenbow, Calgary, Alberta, and Etnografiska Museet, Stockholm, 1854.2.27. **142, 143:** Cumberland County Historical Society, Carlisle, Pennsylvania, neg. no. PA-CH2-12. **144, 145:** Larry Sherer, courtesy Buffalo Gallery, Inc. (2). **146:** Photograph by Florence Pulford, *Morning Star Quilts,* © 1989, Leone Publications, Mountain View, California. **147:** Photograph by Tom Moulin, *Morning Star Quilts,* © 1989, Leone Publications, Mountain View, California. **148:** Vancouver Public Library, photograph no. 9429. **149:** David E. Jones. **150:** Courtesy the Glenbow Archives, Calgary, Alberta, NA1463-16. **151:** Masco Collection. **153:** NAA, Smithsonian Institution, neg. no. 76-13369. **154:** Photo by Wyatt Davis, courtesy Museum of New Mexico, neg. no. 68362; catalog no. 48064/12 Blackware Jar, Maria Martinez, San Ildefonso Pueblo. Blair Clark, photographer. Museum of Indian Arts & Culture/Laboratory of Anthropology, Santa Fe. **156, 157:** Larry Sherer, courtesy Buffalo Gallery, Inc. (2). **159-161:** Dennis L. Sanders. **162, 163:** Delores Twohatchet (2). **164, 165:** James Schnepf/Gamma Liaison. **166, 167:** Yin-May Lee —Susanne Page. **168:** Paul S. Conklin. **169:** Paul S. Conklin—Yin-May Lee. **170:** Paul S. Conklin. **171-175:** Susanne Page. **176:** Rose Palmisano; Susanne Page, and Edward T. Hall—Herbert Lotz. **177:** Yin-May Lee (4).

INDEX